Annalise –
thank you for
attending Literari'
Delights!
♥

REALIZING RIVER CITY

MELISSA GRUNOW

Melissa Grunow
5/20/17

REALIZING RIVER CITY
MELISSA GRUNOW

Tumbleweed Books
Tumble through the pages of our books

HTTP://TUMBLEWEEDBOOKS.CA
An imprint of DAOwen Publications

Realizing River City / Melissa Grunow

ISBN 978-1-928094-22-7
EISBN 978-1-928094-16-6

This is a work of non-fiction. In recounting the events in this memoir,
chronologies have been compressed or altered and details have been changed
to assist the narrative. Where dialogue appears, the intention was to re-create
the essence of conversations rather than verbatim quotes. Names and
identifying characteristics of some individuals have been changed.

Edited by Douglas Owen and MJ Moores
Cover art by Indigo Forest Designs

10 9 8 7 6 5 4 3 2

A deeply rich meditation on what it means to be a woman in a sometimes uncertain and complicated world, in relationship to men, but ultimately, and more importantly, to oneself. Melissa Grunow's *Realizing River City* raises just as many questions as it answers, circling back always, in beautiful prose and a clear, honest voice, to what it means to be alive, to love, and to be present for all of it.

—Amina Cain, author of *Creature* and *I Go to Some Hollow*

Empowering. Beautiful. Brave. These three words are the epitome of Melissa Grunow's *Realizing River City*. Traversing through personal transformations, the strength that lives within her memoir stems from Grunow's fresh writing and unrelenting honesty. She doesn't hold back when showing us the complexities of what it means and what it looks like to become an independent woman. This is a book about liberation. This is a book about revolution. This is a book that will live in your body long after you have finished it, a book that will embolden your life, always.

—Chelsey Clammer, author of *BodyHome*

Realizing River City is the compelling story of Melissa Grunow's search for love with all the wrong men. It's a story about loss, love, compassion, and finally redemption, as Grunow learns to stand on her own, embrace life's messiness, and forge ahead full of hope for the future. I was cheering for her as I turned the final pages!

—Kate Hopper, author of *Ready for Air* and *Use Your Words*

In her memoir *Realizing River City*, Melissa Grunow shares with honesty and clarity the often-precarious landscape of love, loss, and longing. Her book offers readers vibrant details of New Mexico and an intimate glimpse into a woman's persistent search for acceptance and positive relationships.

—Dinty W. Moore, author of *Crafting the Personal Essay*

Melissa Grunow has written an intimate exploration of need, desire, doubt, and survival; her memoir is remarkable for its heart-breaking honesty.

—Robert Root, author of *Happenstance* and *Postscripts: Retrospections on Time and Place*

For Madison

Prologue
Truth or Consequences, New Mexico

I am the first off the bus, eager to start my trip down the river. It's my last day in Truth or Consequences, New Mexico, where I spent the past two weeks as an Artist in Residence to work on my writing without the interruptions and distractions of home or life back in Michigan. The retreat center is made up of four apartments; mine is the one closest to the gate and farthest from the Wi-Fi, a remoteness that cajoles me out of the relentlessly hot apartment each day and to the comparably hot lone café that makes its scones from scratch.

The repetition of walking, working, thinking, and sleeping in the heat has left me feeling tapped, dried up, and tuckered out. This quiet desert town is compressed by the heat, and the people are constantly squinting and feeling melted in the sun that always finds its way in. It's thirsty; I'm thirsty. A Midwestern girl can't thrive in the desert. A day on the Rio Grande River would restore me.

Captain Bob, his tanned and worn skin contrasting against bright yellow shorts, hands me a life jacket after I yank a giant tube off his trailer.

"You'll need this," he says, and motions for me to take it.

Having grown up around Michigan lakes and backyard pools, I know how to swim. I have floated down dozens of rivers in northern Michigan, mostly in canoes, often on some spectrum of drunk, and I have never worn a life jacket. I want to snicker and scoff at his suggestion, but it's his tube and his river, so it's his rules. Setting aside my unfettered arrogance, I put on the life jacket but don't take the time to buckle it before wading out into the water. Pushing the tube in front of me, I wait until the water is up to my thighs before scrambling on top and scooting myself into the seat.

The river is dark and murky. It's so dark that I can't see below the surface or my reflection. My vanity, though, is ephemeral. I'm too hot in this heavenly wasteland to wear my hair down, to layer my face with makeup. Instead, my skin is shiny with sweat. It's pink from two weeks in the desert sun, chubbier than it was a year ago, and more aged and lined than it was ten years ago. I was in my early twenties then, newly married, and a desert transplant trying to make sense of tumbleweeds causing flat tires, cockroaches as common as houseflies, and years without seasons. Wearing those ten years openly on my face, the time heavy on my skin, I look away from the water. I don't want to see myself.

I paddle a little to get ahead of the two other groups behind me, the tube turns around a bend, and then the soundtrack of life stops. No cars. No voices. No music. Nothing. There is only the sound of trickling water, and only when I move my fingertips through the river below me.

It's mid-morning, and I am alone.

Too quickly, the current carries me to the side of the river, and an angry mesquite thorn rips open the skin on my shoulder. A rookie mistake. On Michigan's rivers, bushes taunt from the banks, but they're mostly harmless. They may scratch or poke, but none have ever cut me open. The mesquite gash quickly turns pink and swells, so I press it lightly with the tip of my finger; it's hot to my touch. I pull the flip-flops off my feet and slide them onto my palms to help paddle and steer myself back to the river's center.

I spread my fingers wide and dip them into the water, trailing my arm along the side of the tube as I move with the current. Above me there is sky and then more sky. There are no clouds morphing into shapes and telling stories. As a child, I would lie on the grass at the top of a hill down the street from my house and watch the same sky, always looking for something more than what was there, but my questions remained unanswered. The sky lets me down on the river as well, and I shift my gaze to the space around me that changes as the tube floats on, but stays strangely the same.

On my second night in New Mexico, I had barbecue sauce-covered beef rib slabs smoked for two hours with mesquite wood that we cut from bushes growing in the mountains. We stood around the patio table and sucked meat off the bones like brutes, sauce dripping down our chins and onto thin T-shirts, discarding the carcass in piles. We didn't speak. I hadn't eaten any kind of meat in years. The desert tells a different kind of truth.

I don't want to leave tomorrow. I try to speak the words aloud, but the sound of my voice, of any voice, seems like a disruption to serenity, and I don't want to ruin what has taken me into its tranquility. It's not so much that I don't want to leave as it is that I don't want to return to Michigan, to a house that has sat empty in my absence. There are uninhabited drawers in my bedroom and space in my closet, emptiness that used to be occupied by the belongings of one man or another, some who overstayed their welcome, others who moved on too soon. It's vacant. There is no love, no life, in that home anymore.

Up ahead, I see two ducks wrestling, wings flapping lividly, but neither flies away. That exact place, that exact moment on the water, belongs to both of them and neither of them. The river doesn't stop moving. There is no place. Space is limitless.

On the river, I have nothing. No keys. No identification. No, that's not true. I have sunglasses. Sunglasses that I barely save as they're ripped from my face when I hit a rapid that tosses me off my tube and into the river. The bubbling waves, tall and dark, rise up and form a wall. I saw it up ahead and went right for it anyway. The life jacket tugs and pulls away from my body. It's too late to buckle the straps. The water is cool on my face, and I try not to breathe in as it burns inside my nose and down my throat. I gasp instead of scream. The tube passes over my head, tugging hair loose from my pony-tail. The lifejacket tries to pull me to the surface, but it billows at my neck, trapped by my chin, and it chokes me.

Nobody knows I'm here.

My nose feels tender, and I fear it's bleeding. I kick and struggle to hoist myself back up. The current is too fast, though, and my legs buoy beneath the tube, knees bumping up against the bottom, my head goes under again. Weeds tickle and taunt my body as I float hidden below the river's surface; rocks scrape my skin. I cannot lift myself up, and the tube is too big, too heavy, the material made to withstand the mesquite thorns. Unable to let it go, I can't hang onto to it, either. The current picks up, and the tube forces my head under water, again. I don't know which way to the surface. The light, the blur of river water in my eyes, the fabric of the tube and the moss on the rocks all spin me, turn me. I am in a room without a door.

Maybe this is why I have returned to this desert town, to the river that shares a sky with my childhood home, away from a place where love has dried up and said good-bye to me long ago. I wouldn't, couldn't do this to myself, couldn't invite in the darkness, but maybe I could let it happen. Maybe this is what I was heading toward all along, all the times that love and loss and longing and regret crippled me. All it would take is one deep breath. One deep breath and it would be over. The sun blurs in the water around me, and I stop kicking, stop grasping, stop tugging at the floppy life jacket. I stop struggling, ready to surrender.

PART I

WADING

Chapter One

"*Señiorita*, come inside! Have something cold to drink."

I paused, but only for a second. He squinted in the sunlight and flashed a broad, white smile, and I felt instant trust in a city of untrustworthy men. I hadn't planned to stop for lunch, but couldn't deny that a mango Jumex or a strawberry margarita on this hot, early June day sounded like a good idea. So I followed the waiter into the cantina, dropped my purse onto an empty chair, and rested my elbows on the mosaic tile tabletop while he sprinted off to fetch a menu.

The man behind the counter at the *farmacia* had just tried to sell me antibiotics because he didn't understand that I wanted birth control pills. My Spanish had always been terrible, but his English was worse. The last time I visited Ciudad Juárez my husband was with me, and I was able to slink behind him as he did all the navigating and negotiating, the dialect purring in his throat while he interacted with the locals as if he were one of them. I would pretend to browse the pharmaceuticals beneath the glass countertop hoping it wasn't too obvious I only understood every fourth or fifth word, the exchange between them too fast for my two years of high school Spanish to keep up.

When John and I first moved from Michigan to Las Cruces, day trips to Juárez were adventures of cultural discovery. We would stroll into little makeshift shops along the alleys to look at the trinkets, the knick-knacks, the handmade jewelry, the serapes, ponchos, tunics, and cowboy boots. I even had a few of those Mexican souvenirs decorating my apartment: ceramic, colorful, hand-painted, spur-of-the-moment purchases for which we had to haggle down to almost fifty percent of the asking price. Shopping in Juárez was an activity of persistence and focus. There was no such thing as browsing; if I expressed even the slightest interest in an object, the shop keeper pursued the sale throughout the store until I finally hoofed it outside to move on where the next clerk was ready to pounce.

For three months, my husband had been my ex-husband, and so when it came time for a day trip to Juárez, I decided to go alone. With the anticipation that my office flirtation with a younger man named Raul would soon get physical, and no health insurance provided by my employer, I had no choice but to take myself across the bridge and into a country that made no distinction between prescription and over-the-counter drugs. I could buy birth control as easily as I could buy Ibuprofen.

My mom called while I had been driving the streets of downtown El Paso looking for a cheap parking spot. We chatted for almost fifteen minutes before I dropped into the conversation about leaving the country for the afternoon. "For souvenir shopping," I told her. A lie. She wouldn't want to hear the truth.

Although I had lived in the desert for four years, my parents never visited me. Their perception of my southern New Mexico home was one of desolation, cockroaches, *cholo* gang violence, and poverty. They couldn't imagine what I saw every day: the palm tree-lined streets in front of adobe-style houses against a jagged mountain backdrop. It was peaceful and picturesque, but they never learnt that for themselves.

"Be careful," she sighed. She knew it was pointless to try and dissuade me.

However, an hour away in the border town of Juárez, her warning would be appropriate if she knew of the *feminicidios*—female killings—that had been happening long before I relocated to New Mexico. I knew women were abducted, sometimes in daylight, and later found raped, tortured, and mutilated, their bodies dumped in public places. It was a risk to be a woman alone in Juárez. A single woman seeking birth control in a country whose faith worshipped saints and virgins was in direct defiance of the traditional machismo culture in a city controlled by a hyper-masculine drug cartel.

But my mother didn't actually know any of this. To her, a foreign country was a foreign country, and the dangers were no more extreme in Juárez than they would be in a London pub or a voodoo-practicing village in Ghana. For me, the trip was more than just an effort to score birth control. It was the first desert adventure without a husband. For the better part of our first year together I didn't even drive my car because where I went, he went. There was no shaking him. To go to Juárez alone was an opportunity for me to experience the desert through my desires, not his.

It was at least a mile walk in direct sunlight from the parking garage at the El Paso Convention Center to the Bridge of the Americas that connected El Paso to Juárez. Along the way, buildings changed from old, detailed architecture to concrete boxes; their peeled paint advertised the services offered inside the gated door. The closer I got to the bridge, the more the retail moved onto the sidewalk: dusty tables piled with sunglasses, kitchen appliances, knit caps, shoes, and clothing in a kind of pseudo-open air market. The Spanish became thicker and more common with each block, and my white skin practically glowed against a backdrop of dusty, dark buildings.

The journey across the bridge took effort as the climb was steep and hurried, never allowing pedestrians to dawdle or linger because hesitation drew the attention of beggars and pick-pockets. When I saw men trying to sell windshield visors to drivers who were stopped in traffic on the multi-lane bridge, I knew I had crossed into Mexico because such a practice was illegal in the U.S.

There were two-foot-tall coils of barbed wire over the bridge wall that caught shopping bags in their spikes and shredded them. I watched those plastic ribbons fight in the wind, and far below saw concrete irrigation ditches that once contained the Rio Grande. The water dissipated, the only thing to see was the concrete spray-painted with graffiti. The city, like the river, had dried up and left little in its place.

Along the way, women sat on the filthy concrete, holding a plastic cup or basket, their hand out in front of them, muttering in Spanish. Many of them held babies or young children on their laps. They looked dirty, tired, and poorly fed. I slid my hand into a front pocket and touched the quarters and edges of dollar bills.

"Don't flash your money around!" I heard my ex-husband's voice as clearly as if he were walking next to me, the sweat collecting in the center of his back and bleeding through his T-shirt. "You'll draw attention to yourself."

As if my pink-white skin and German heritage hadn't already. I would fall a step behind him and attempt to be discrete as I tossed a quarter into a basket. He always turned back at the moment the coin left my open hand and fell into another. A scowl crept across his face as his ever-hunching shoulders tensed atop his broad back. This happened every time we went to Juárez. Every time he scolded me for parting with a coin, and every time I ignored him. A small but significant act of defiance.

The morning my marriage ended, I woke up early, went into the laundry room to feed our cats, then went back to bed. That's when John rolled over to face me, our heads on our own pillows, our eyes on each other.

"I think this is the end," I said.

There was no argument. Not anymore. We had argued enough about too many things for too long. There was nothing left.

He wasn't concerned about what would happen to me, if I would be okay. Either he wasn't worried, or he didn't care. I was too scared to know, so I didn't ask. Married at twenty-one and divorced by twenty-five, I didn't really know how to be an adult without a partner.

We spent that weekend dividing our belongings, and I didn't cry until I had to separate Christmas ornaments. We didn't even have a Christmas tree.

John only had one question. "What are we going to do about the cats?"

Without him to lead the way in Juárez my legs didn't stop moving me forward, though I was stiffened with anxiety about who and where I was, and that the "who" and the "where" had never mixed before without an escort. A moment of doubt made me wonder if a day trip to Juárez was really the best way to acclimate to my new sense of self-reliance.

When I got to the end of the bridge, I stepped through the gate and onto the dusty Juárez road which gave off a syrupy and sour-rancid smell, like the aftermath of a carnival. But the circus never left Juárez.

Leaning against a building, a man whistled a catcall in my direction. I angled my chin upward and stiffened my back as I walked a little faster. Every third storefront was a *farmacia,* and the men behind the counters stood on the sidewalk and hustled when business was slow, advertising Viagra mostly, in quiet, pushy, accented voices. I passed by them without making eye contact. Most of them were small, even shorter than me, yet their lurking left me unsettled. Their presence forced me to step to the edge of the sidewalk, and I still felt as though they were crowding me, closing in on me. I soon crossed the street to the next block, and finally got up the nerve to cross a threshold.

The white walls and clean glass countertops in the *farmacia* were a stark contrast against the dirty streets. I told the man in a lab coat behind the counter that I wanted birth control, and he laid out four different packages of pills in front of me.

"Choose," he said.

They were familiar brands sold in the U.S. as well. *"Cuánto cuesta?"*

When he told me the cheapest was twenty dollars a pack, I asked for others. "*Nunca más*," he said, and so I left. The ones I was looking for were only sold in Mexico and only cost five dollars. Although nervous, I wouldn't allow a crooked pharmacist to deceive me.

Another two blocks, and I could barely see the height of the bridge behind me. I wandered into another *farmacia* and wished I knew the translation for birth control as the pharmacist tapped the lid of the antibiotics bottles. "For infection," he said.

I shook my head. "*Para no niños.*" I waved my hands in front of my stomach.

The pharmacist chuckled, set the antibiotics under the counter, and produced the box of pills I recognized.

I asked for twelve.

He raised his eyebrows, "*Doce?*"

"*Por favor,*" I replied, and started counting out cash to show him I was serious.

I left the *farmacia* and stopped long enough to stand in front of a trash can, take the pill packs out of their boxes, stash them in deep pockets in my purse, and discard the containers. There would be just three boxes in my bag to show the border checkpoint agent because that was the maximum number I was allowed to bring back into the United States at one time.

During my first visit to Juárez, I hid all the pill packs in my purse, feigning I had just been a tourist for the day. Instead, I learned quickly they only become suspicious of you if you don't have any shopping bags, and so each time thereafter I claimed the three-month limit on the birth control when passing through. Sweat rolled down the back of my neck, and my jeans clung to my warm thighs. I was ready to go home. Walking back to the bridge, I was approached by a waiter.

"*Señorita*, come inside! Have something to drink."

He plopped a menu in front of me, and I struggled to read the Spanish descriptions below each item. A few minutes later he came back, laughed, and changed out the menu for another written in English. Intended to be an act of thoughtful awareness, it slapped me with the truth I had felt all day, I didn't belong there. That was what it really meant to be an outsider, for people to be divided by bridges and rivers and languages, as well as a sense of security and personal safety.

Soon after being seated, a *mariachi* trio walked in and approached the tables, offering performances for a price. A woman requested they play while she sang. Although she was in a different section of the restaurant, her voice lifted above the cigarette smoke to the back where I sat. Her melody was rich, colorful, and pristine. She continued for four or five songs as I watched the waiters dart around the restaurant, never stopping once.

My waiter returned and asked me if I wanted anything else. I shook my head and reached for my wallet.

"Relax, *Señiorita*. Relax."

So I did. I looked through the front door and saw two men sitting on the street, bandannas shielding their heads from the sun, their boot-covered feet stretched out in front of them, hands weathered and dirty.

Outside, people didn't move very fast. There were no jobs in the border town, so men with engineering degrees resorted to selling snack-sized bags of chips off a cart on the street just to house their families. Some men had earned enough to buy their own cars and used them as a taxi service to take American tourists to the Mercado. Some men became waiters, others sold wares in back alley shops. Those who didn't know English were left begging in the streets because they couldn't cater to American tourists; people with money. People like me.

But not really me. Part of my guilt when I went to Juárez was knowing what a fraud I was. It hadn't been so long ago that I was like the dirty children who roamed the street without supervision. I knew what it was like to not have those excess dollar bills that passed from my sweaty hand to a skinny one. In Mexico, and in other aspects of my adult life, I masqueraded as something other than who I had been growing up. I learnt how to pass, to blend in.

A child with dark straight hair, big eyes, filthy clothes, and no shoes, wandered into the restaurant. She walked up to tables with her hand out. Some people gave her quarters while other people shooed her away. When she approached my table, she muttered something, her words quick and quiet, and she took a grubby finger and touched the leftover food on my plate.

Horrified, I raised my hand as if to strike her, responding the way people would to a disobedient dog that was audacious enough to eat off the table. "What are you doing?" The question was almost a shout. She never looked up at me; she never flinched.

The child moved her fingers away from the plate, but kept her eyes focused on the food. Something shifted inside me, and I lowered my hand to my lap. I sat back in the seat as my heartbeat began to slow to normal. Picking up half of my quesadilla, I offered it to her. She took it in one hand and the quarter I gave her in the other. My heart softened a little more as salsa dropped onto her frock. I pointed to an empty chair, "*¿Quieres sentarte?*" I asked. *Would you like to sit down?*

She reminded me of my sister as a child. We would bully her, my brother and me. She had a "blankie" and dragged it behind her all over the house when she was about three or so, shortly after my mom left us, before my dad remarried and had two more children, both boys, putting my sister in the middle of five kids in a family with no money.

My sister would sleep with her blankie, eat with it wrapped around her shoulders, wrap her dolls in it, and use it as a towel after she took a bath. The satin trim eventually started to unravel. My brother and I would pull on it and make it rip, tearing the trim in pieces, pieces my sister would grab out of our hands, put in the middle of the blanket and fold the edges over it, as if that would put it back together. We would laugh. We were mean. We liked to make my sister cry.

It was fun because it was easy, and we didn't have cable. If something was broken or missing, we blamed her. Our faces somber, our heads would nod together. "Mary Beth did it," we would lie. We let her suffer the spankings, even if my dad whipped her in front of us. It wasn't right, but that was what you did when you were just a child yourself, you were scared, and you were angry with and envious of everyone around you.

The child in the restaurant had my sister's countenance and some of her demeanor. She was quiet but not shy. Like my sister, she was sneaky, skinny, and tan, and had narrow feet, the toes just a little too long. Her eyes were big, but she didn't look at me with them. Instead, she kept them focused on what she wanted. She made me feel pity for her, but she also stirred in me the same prevalence for violence I felt toward my sister growing up. It was as if that child, my sister, had crossed some unseen, unnamed, and until that moment, unfelt boundary that teased the very primitive aspect of my nature. Her behavior made me flare up with irritation and the irrational desire to strike another human being. Even if that person was just a hungry child who only wanted a quarter, or who only wanted to keep her blankie intact.

"*¿Quieres sentarte?*" I asked the girl again. I didn't know if my question was understood until she shook her head and was off, sauntering toward the door, her bare feet silent against the cool tile.

The margarita had melted into warm syrup in the bottom of my glass, but I swallowed the rest of it down anyway. As I made my way to the door, the waiter didn't say goodbye to me. He had already moved on, already recruited a few more people, some couples this time, to go inside and have something to drink.

Making my way across the bridge, my calves started to burn and quiver from the uphill climb. The quarters rested comfortably against my thigh in my jeans pocket. Being a woman, I was warned about Juárez all the time. There were faces of missing women printed on fliers and posted on pillars all along the walk back to the border checkpoint. With my vision on the exit I wasn't afraid anymore, but just in case, I walked with fierce determination. There was dirt in my nostrils and my teeth from the dust that always blew; the desert sands were as ruthless as the sun.

Up ahead, I saw a woman with a child lying across her lap. I looked at him and saw he was incredibly still, his eyes a little vacant, bored, and staring up over his head, just out of his line of sight. Could it be the heat or was he hungry? Was he just a quiet child, or was it something worse, something spare change couldn't fix?

The woman's stretch-marked belly hung over the top of her pants. Her long hair was pulled back into a messy, frizzy ponytail. I didn't have any dollar bills in my hand, so I reached into my pocket, wrapped my first around three of the four quarters and dropped them into her basket. I didn't hear them land. I only heard her quiet, tired *muchas gracias* as I made my way to the customs checkpoint, hoping my shifting stare and distracted expression wouldn't give them good enough reason to search the zippered pockets inside my purse.

Chapter Two

I have to get out of this city. In the weeks that followed my trip to Juárez, I had worked long hours, after which I went home, feed the cat (my half of the divorce settlement), and then trekked across town to Raul's apartment.

Our casual chats over interoffice IM had quickly progressed to playing cards in the break room, to chats in the parking lot at the end of the day, to IMs at home. Some nights I stopped by to drop something off—oven mitts because he didn't have any, strawberry jelly because he accidentally bought grape. Soon he invited me over a few times a week, and finally I was at his apartment every day, the invitation perpetual and implied.

Stretching out across his bed, I watched him play video games or listened to him narrate the chat room exchanges with old high school friends. When it got late, he climbed into bed next to me and promptly fell asleep. I stayed awake for hours afterward, a dark ceiling above me, the hum of the computer fan from across the room the only sound, a failed attempt at lulling me to sleep. Sometimes I watched Raul snooze and wondered how to classify our relationship. It wasn't something I could ask him to define for me.

We were friends, I suppose. Friends who shared a bed, but not each other.

*

Raul came into my life when I was brand new to my position writing technical manuals for a software development company. There was chemistry between us even though I couldn't figure out what initially drew me to him. He wasn't particularly attractive. Tall, of course, and Latino, his skin tone a smooth, almost caramel color. He was younger than I, by about four years, but his overweight body wasn't aging well. His hair was thinning, even in his early twenties. He dressed more like a used car salesman than his own peers. His sense of humor was terribly immature and he believed himself to be much smarter than those around him. Being an introvert and a recluse enabled him to be the ruler of his own tiny world; it was a world I longed to infiltrate.

From the beginning, he made it clear he wasn't interested in me because I wasn't good enough for him. I was thin, but not thin enough.

"Suck in that brisket," he would tell me as he poked my stomach. My hair was long, but not long enough. "My ex had hair all the way down her back." I was a woman, but not feminine enough. "Why don't you ever paint your nails?" I was too pale, too stumpy, too opinionated, but also too competitive. When his endless lusting after Jodi—a divorcée twice his age—evolved into an afternoon of sex in her bedroom ("She leaves the television on," he said. "Isn't that weird?"), I knew if she could be convinced, then he could be convinced. I pined for him without shame simply because I couldn't have him, like a middle school girl who desires a high school boy.

At work, he was an Internet junkie who would send me links to videos, websites, comics, and—when he was talking down to me—definitions of words that he thought I didn't understand. The expectation was to laugh. Everyone laughed at his humor or risked being the victim of it. I tried to find the delicate balance between giving him the attention he needed so he wouldn't turn his dark humor on me and concentrating on my editing projects, hoping the endless distractions wouldn't make my work sloppy and get me fired.

He also had moments of kindness, of thoughtfulness, moments where I felt connected to him because he said something insightful or did something unexpected. Moments where he would ask me questions when I took time off work to visit family.

"How was your trip home? You look relaxed today," he noticed when I returned. Moments like the time we were out playing darts with other co-workers, and he fixed the tip on my set so I could finally hit and stick the board. He confided in me when he drove all night to the center of Texas to see a crush from a high school. "Do you think she's interested? What should I say? What should I do?"

Raul had me hooked on the hope that I would catch him being a good person, that I would be witness to a different sort of man, a better man than how he presented himself to everyone else. My marriage had failed, and Raul was the first man in five years to pay me any attention. I was desperate for his attention, desperate to know for sure I hadn't made a mistake in ending a marriage to a man who had only wondered if the divorce—not the wedding—had been a mistake. Raul gave me a chance to test my decision, to enable me to stop second-guessing myself. So instead of discounting him, I pursued him.

Winter was over in New Mexico. The shortest season of the year, it passed without incident, without heavy down coats, without much disruption to the patterns of daily life. One day the trees had leaves, and the next they didn't. The temperature dropped fifteen degrees, the wind picked up, and it stayed that way for three months.

It was during one of those chilly winter days when Raul tugged at my sweater, gestured for a condom, and pulled me on top of him. I fumbled then held my breath with eyes closed. It should have happened naturally, but it was anything but natural. It felt different and new, as though I had never done it before.

Bracing myself, I clutched the sheets on either side of his head as my wrists bore all the weight. When I repositioned myself onto my forearms, he turned his face away from mine and stared at the wall until it was over. I was both acutely and subconsciously aware that agreeing to this physical relationship meant it was okay for him to use me. Trading my emotions for his affection was a type of love whoring that I wasn't prepared to deal with.

A week later, it was past ten o'clock at night and the entire office staff worked against a deadline to deliver the beta version of our software to a client. The programming team kept finding bugs in their code, and I couldn't finish the User Guide until they worked out the kinks. The lead programmers huddled together in their workspace in the center of the main room, Raul sat off to the side, and I was hidden in a back office taking screen shots and writing instructions with each new update.

My office messenger indicator lit up and flashed incessantly in the lower right corner of my screen. Raul was bored. The only way to make it stop was to click on it, but I didn't have time to get into a conversation with him. Raul, as always, was relentless. He sent repeated attention-getters of "hey" and links to random websites, websites he had sent me before, websites with silly videos, but I was too tired to laugh.

Finally, a new message popped up on my computer screen, the words dreaded, yet inevitable.

"I just want to be friends. It was a mistake."

I stared the words down, and couldn't fake shock, not even to myself. For whatever reason, I repulsed him. For me, our night together had been progress toward something real. For him, it had been a lapse in judgment.

Melissa Grunow

A mistake.

"I agree," I lied to him and to myself. "We're better off as friends."

After clicking back to the document, I edited the final pages with blurry eyes and a reddening nose, inwardly pleading that no one would wander into my office, that I could stay hidden in the corner, a protective wall between me and the others. I didn't want to forever be known as "The girl who cried at work" or answer any questions of concern or intrusiveness.

His message indicator was quiet for a while. Every few minutes I clicked over, typed a paragraph to him confessing my desire to be with him, my plea for him to give me a chance, that we could be good together. Too bruised for another ricochet of rejection, I would let it sit for a moment then promptly delete it.

It's time to get out of this city. A week after we delivered the finished software, I was scheduled for vacation. Since I had worked many hours of overtime, I could afford a last-minute plane ticket out of town. But where to go? That night, I scrolled though my list of contacts and fired off an email to Ian, a classmate since the fourth grade. He lived in Las Vegas, just a two-hour and two-hundred-dollar flight away. Ian agreed to host me, and three days later, I scanned the swarm of faces at the baggage claim until I found his.

That first night Ian took me to Fremont Street, the Strip for the Locals, he called it. We walked up and down the street with large, frothy draft beers in our hands and just talked. Ian perpetuated the conversation by asking questions, I perpetuated by answering them and tried to reminisce about our days in school together—elementary, middle, high school, and college—even though we hadn't had much interaction after high school graduation.

Whenever I told a story that began, "Do you remember…" he shrugged.

"To be honest," he finally said. "I don't really remember you." He asked me if I was trying to walk him to death as he directed me to a stool in an open-air bar. We sat down together and he tried to flag down the bartender.

I stared at him and felt the pull in my gut I would often feel when Raul dismissed me in some way. "You don't?"

"I mean, I remember going to school with you. But were we actually friends? Did we hang out?"

12

He was right. We hadn't really known each other.

"I guess not," I said. "We were friendly, but I guess it wasn't more than that."

Ian was quiet for a moment, and then sat up straight and smiled. "But we're friends now," he said. "So that's pretty cool."

I smiled, accepting the situation for what it was. He had a way of making me feel at ease and likeable. I didn't have to beg him to consider my thoughts or my words. He took me into his home without question, without me needing to explain my desperation in getting away from a hopeless, volatile situation.

The next day we decided to have a tourist night in Vegas, spending time on the Strip, stopping at the Bellagio fountains, MGM lion head, and other novelties for photos. Dressed head-to-toe in black, I strapped on a pair of chunky-heeled sandals, straightened my hair, and darkened my eyes. I was ready.

While walking along the Las Vegas strip next to Ian, I kept my bag on the side of my body away from the street. We had just stopped at a fountain for pictures, and I could feel the back spray as water connected with water, a mist that cooled us just slightly on a warm summer evening. I didn't mind that the mist might frizz my hair because every time I turned toward Ian, he smiled, no matter how I looked.

The street was crowded with people edging past one another. Signs along the way warned against j-walking, threatening citations from the Las Vegas police, as cars inched along, crowding all lanes of the street that wove between the sprawl of casinos, showrooms, and restaurants boasting $4.99 prime rib dinners. The crowd pressed on, not allowing me to pause long enough to marvel at the base of the Eifel Tower and wonder how much it was dwarfed by the real thing in Paris. There were so many lights around us that I barely remembered it was evening. I tripped a little from staring up instead of looking ahead, and Ian steadied me with sideways glance and a chuckle.

"We haven't even started drinking yet," he mused.

Up ahead, the crowd shifted in a snake-like motion, the bobbing of heads following suit as they slithered around an object on the sidewalk. Then just beyond the Eifel Tower replica, I saw a young police officer with a notepad in his hand talking to a small group of people seated on the sidewalk, their backs against a concrete wall.

"Okay, who saw it?" The officer looked from face to face.

"I didn't see it," someone remarked, "but I heard it."

There was a man lying face down on the ground, one arm above his head, the other next to his body, as if he were trying to swim across the sidewalk. He looked crumpled, flattened almost. To my right was a stopped car, a giant hole in the windshield with long cracks inching away from it like the roots of a tree. The driver's seat was empty, the silent car an anomaly on the smog-ridden street.

Rolling away from the man was a trickle of blood so dark it was almost black. The blood flowed in a single rivulet down the sidewalk and pooled next to his knee. I had never seen blood that dark, a body so flat, muscles so still. It wasn't until I stepped over his ankle and continued down the street that I realized he was dead.

I turned my head to look back at him, and met Ian's eyes halfway there. People continued to crowd behind and alongside us, the dead man quickly forgotten by this city, the keeper of secrets.

"Are you okay?" Ian's concern was genuine.

I removed a hand from my gaping mouth and nodded. But I didn't need to speak. The lights around us continued to flash, the slot machines chimed from inside the casino doors, and yet, in that moment, Vegas had lost some of its light.

"I hate the Strip," he said. It was all he could say. We crossed a bridge, careful to stay on the pedestrian path as cars whizzed past and below us, the headlights jousting with the bright bulbs from the signage, the buildings, the fountains, and the billboards. Yet, I felt trapped in darkness, in a shadow that had settled in the city around us.

"Tomorrow—" I started.

"Tomorrow," he responded. "We're going to see a different side of Nevada. I hope you brought your hiking shoes."

*

It felt like a dream, but it wasn't. Seated on a giant boulder, Ian somewhere among the rocks below me, I opened my eyes to the desert sun. Red sand stretched for miles in front of me, a rolling field of frozen fire. It was vastly different from the summer bonfires I enjoyed while growing up in Michigan, and yet there was something about it that was so strikingly similar it made me long for establishing my own traditions in New Mexico, something to look forward to as the seasons slowly and mildly shifted one into the next.

Instead, I had spent my time there splitting myself between learning to be a good wife to a man who didn't know how to be a husband, and auditioning to be a girlfriend for a man who didn't know how to love anyone besides himself. There had been no room, and no place, for me.

I climbed up on top of a plateaued bolder at Red Rock Canyon, just to see if I could while wearing black lace-ups with thick, two-inch heels better suited for a dance floor than a hike in the wilderness. Because I had only packed heels and sandals, I went with the shoes that had a better chance of staying on my feet.

I scooted to the edge of the rock, dangled my feet over the side, raised my arms into the air, and smiled for the camera in Ian's hand. A chubby ten-year-old crossed my path on the way back down. The girl scooted along, inching herself forward on her behind.

She looked over at me as we passed each other and said, "I can't believe you're wearing high-heels."

She crouched in front of me, waiting for a response. I looked that child up and down, and then scanned the perimeter for an adult who could be her parent.

Finding no one, I said, "You're wearing flip-flops." I paused to see if she would deny it. She didn't. "And *a skirt*. So shut your mouth."

At the base of the rock, Ian helped me down since I couldn't jump comfortably in my shoes and asked me, "Did you just get into a fight with a first-grader?"

I shrugged. "I blame the desert. It tells a different kind truth."

He scoffed an Ian chuckle. "How many kinds are there?"

"Well." I hoisted myself up onto a plateau. "There's truth. Then there's the hard truth, the real truth, the kind that everyone knows, and nobody wants to hear." I turned my face toward the sky and squinted at the sun. Ian acknowledged my distinction with a flick of his chin before holding out his hand to help me down.

We continued walking throughout the park, away from the boulders and toward the various cactus plants that managed to thrive under the unrelenting sun, the ones that grow thorns as long and thick as my fingers. My chunky shoes kicked up gravel and dust as we hiked the trail in silence. We hadn't brought water or supplies; we didn't really need them. It was warm, but we weren't hot, the sun almost refreshing after a few days of living only at night. The cuffs of my pants caught on my heels and split a little at the seams. The pants were baggier than the last time I had worn them, and they hung loose away from my body. I felt small and light along that trail, free. My choices, my body, belonged to me there.

Approaching a bend in the trail, we happened upon a small stream, no more than a few inches deep and two feet wide, cutting its way into the sand and twisting around pebbles – an oasis for the greenery thriving on its banks.

Ian nudged the waterline with his toe. "Where did this river come from?"

"Have you had any rain lately?"

He looked at me and grinned. "It's Vegas," he said. "It doesn't rain in this city."

While stepping over the stream, I dragged the pebbles with my heels until the ground was dry. I couldn't help but to think of Raul, how as a married woman, I hadn't expected to meet a man who caught my attention, a man who became the object of my desire so soon after the separation and speedy divorce. He was a river in the desert, unforeseen and therefore fascinating. His appeal was a mystery, as was what he found appealing. I wanted to figure him out, but there were no solutions, no answers to the how and why of him. He just was. The choice to linger and wonder or to move on was mine alone to make.

"Sit over there." Ian pointed to a small boulder on the other side of the stream at the base of a tree-sized bush. "I'll take your picture."

On the last day of my trip, he took me to a casino, handed me twenty dollars and said, "You can't come to Vegas and not do any gambling. It's like a rule." He hadn't allowed me to pay for anything while I was there; meals, drinks, entertainment, he covered it all. Since I was staying at his apartment, I didn't have to pay for a hotel, either. The cash I had stuffed into my wallet before I left was still there, except for the few times I snuck off and bought us both drinks before he could insist on covering the tab.

"I have money."

It was useless to argue. I was his guest, and he insisted that I enjoy a few hits on the slot machines.

"Tell you what," he said. "If you hit the jackpot, then you have to share the winnings with me. Deal?"

I nodded and took the money from his hand. He wandered off to play video poker, and I sat down at a machine and fed it Ian's money. Like everything else in Vegas, the slots sparkled in lights, dinging each time I pushed the button, even when I lost, which was often. I spent half the money and thought about cashing out and moving to a nickel slot or penny slot but knew Ian would tease me for it. He chuckled when I selected a quarter slot machine, shaking his head at my frugality.

"You can't win big if you don't play big," he said before disappearing to bet a dollar at a time, sometimes tripling the bet when he had a good hand.

My hoped-for life with Raul was a gamble, a bet without a marker. I knew I didn't have a future in New Mexico in general or with Raul in particular. Most of my friends were gone; they had either stopped talking to me after the divorce or they had left the state already, moving on to relationships of their own. Some got married, others had babies, most did both.

When Ian dropped me off at the airport, his hug good-bye wasn't lingering, wasn't wrapped in implications, wasn't the start of a transitional romance. Ian wasn't and never would be that guy for me. He made me promise to send him the pictures we took together along the Las Vegas Boulevard and at Red Rock Canyon. He wouldn't know until he received it, that a package would come to him a week later with the pictures burned to a CD, a batch of homemade Rice Krispy treats, and *Chasing Amy* on DVD, a movie we both loved and quoted throughout my visit, our shared moments.

My flight wasn't for two more hours, so I wandered around the terminal, in and out of gift shops, each filled with magazines, pop fiction paperbacks, overpriced bottled water, and shot glasses designed with every stereotype of Las Vegas imaginable. Scanning the racks, I was unwilling to commit to any new purchases I would have to add to my already-full backpack. I passed by a block of slot machines three or four times before finally sitting down at one and fed it a crumpled five-dollar bill. Three wheels of fruit and dollar signs spun like a rotisserie in front of me.

Nothing.

I yanked the lever.

Nothing.

I pulled the lever again.

Still nothing.

I paused and looked around, studying the old and young wandering past me, carrying bags or dragging around wheeled suitcases, hands barely a grip on the handle. Children clung to stuffed animals or dolls, adults clutched the hands of children, or stacks of magazines, or takeout containers full of overpriced food. We were all the same, all on our way to a home, ours or someone else's, moving through our lives without thought as to how we got there or why. We just existed; we settled for what had become normal. All of us may have put down bets in Vegas, but to what extent had we taken a gamble? To what extent would we ever?

Turning back to the slot machine, I pulled the lever one more time. The bells and lights whirled above me as quarters spat out of the base of the machine. Four of them. I had won a dollar, broken even.

After cashing out, I walked to my gate, and sat on the floor against the window until they told me it was time to board. I may not have been ready to leave Ian, but I was ready to go home.

Chapter Three

When I returned to New Mexico after my time in Vegas, I used my first work week to research Ph.D. programs in the Midwest. After delivering our project, my boss had difficulty securing new contracts, and rumors quickly spread to the company's thirty employees that we might shut down entirely in the months to come. I couldn't afford to be without a job, and there wasn't much of a market for writers of any kind in Las Cruces. It was time to move on, both geographically, but even more so, emotionally.

While the trip to Las Vegas had given me confidence, Raul was quick to swoop in and stomp all over me in his muddy boots, though I didn't realize what happened until I was bruised and covered in dirt again. He pulled me back in slowly, steadily, and gradually.

I spent every evening with him in his apartment, ordering in Chinese food or making spaghetti and watching The Simpsons (no re-runs, though. Only new episodes). We grew closer, and it wasn't long before the closeness brought naked bodies together again, over and over. This time, it was not a mistake. This time, he didn't want to remain friends, though he kept me a secret from his buddies and didn't declare us to be anything to his family. I enjoyed his mother's company, the lunches and chats we had together, and even then, there was nothing stated, nothing defined.

My time with Raul was fleeting, and I knew that. Each week I rode the gamut of feeling excited about the changes to come and panicked that we weren't making the best of our time together, wasting the nights we didn't touch or talk or connect.

I didn't talk to him, not about anything important. It wasn't a good idea to ask questions, to demand answers, explanations, and definitely not reassurances. He wasn't in the business of making me feel better. Days where I felt him pulling away were the nights when I stared at the ceiling fan while he slept, disappointment and regret spilling onto the wrinkled pillowcase beneath my head. But then there were days when he would tickle me, smile at me, make me laugh, and not make me cry— those were the days I was able to shop for apartments and moving truck companies, could research travel arrangements that would enable me to bring my cat on the journey across the country. The kinder he was to me, the less I needed him.

Less than a year after I met Raul, and a summer of sleeping with him, I moved from New Mexico to Ohio to start a doctorate program. I loaded a suitcase, air mattress, blankets, and my cat into my car for a trip that would take three days, navigating through parts of Texas, Oklahoma, Missouri, Illinois, Indiana, and finally the center of Ohio.

The New Mexico heat was getting to me even though everyone insisted it was better because it's wasn't as humid as Ohio. I was tired of the bugs: the centipedes and cockroaches and spiders and all the other unidentifiable crawly things that liked to burrow in the bathtub drain until the water that rushed from the showerhead chased them out to circle my feet.

Raul took a few days off of work to ride with me, a generous gesture and a thoughtful way to say good-bye. Even though he criticized my music selections constantly and demanded that I cover the cost of his every meal, I excused his malice and freeloading. He couldn't bring himself to say it, but he didn't want me to leave. Not by my own choices anyway.

"I'm not ready to let you go," he eventually said. It was the first night in my new apartment, before the furniture arrived. We set up the air mattress in the middle of the room and covered it with blankets and pillows dressed with fresh pillowcases. The cat roamed the space around us, occasionally rubbing her head against my hand and licking the fingertips. We had just devoured a takeout container of chicken wings, and without soap, I hadn't gotten all of the flavors off of my skin. She purred, her motor running strong, and tried to curl up with us, but Raul shooed her away. "Can't you lock her in a closet or something?" he asked. "She can't ever be quiet."

"You're not?" I asked, changing the subject back to me—to us. "Too bad you couldn't fly out in a few days instead of tomorrow. My parents will be here in the afternoon to help unload the truck. You could meet them if you were staying."

"That's not what I mean." He stretched out on the air mattress and stared up at the ceiling, always at the ceiling.

"What do you mean?"

He scoffed and rolled his eyes toward me, then away. Here it was again. I couldn't figure out what he meant, and it annoyed him to have to spell it out for me.

"You want to try and make this work?"

"Yeah." He turned toward me, his eyes on mine, but his voice carried a trail of aggravation, and the space between us filled with questions, with doubt.

I spent those first nine months flying in and out of the El Paso airport trying to keep the relationship going, but my efforts often backfired. If I stayed longer than three days during any given visit, we would fight. It normally started with him disapproving of my hairstyle, my clothes, or telling me that I never wore enough makeup to cover the imperfections in my skin. They were the same criticisms over and over until I refused to listen any longer.

When Raul and I fought, we fought without resistance or regret.

"I have really high standards. I deserve better than you," he once said to me. It was four hours into an argument. He was seated at his computer in the corner of the bedroom, hunched forward, elbows resting on knees, his giant frame sinking into itself. Our fights were slaughterhouses of words.

I stood next to his open closet, pulling clothes off the hangers and stuffing them into my rolling duffle bag. Scattered on the floor were objects he had thrown at me when I started packing my bag. They were mostly gifts I gave him and framed pictures of us, memories created where the smiles hid a rigid system of rules I could never seem to follow.

Every few months, I scraped together enough money to fly across the country to the El Paso airport, knowing I couldn't afford it, but doing so anyway because Raul harangued me relentlessly about moving to Ohio in the first place.

"It's your fault, Tubby," he said. "You're the one who left."

I deceived myself for an entire year pretending my relationship was something extraordinary, that it was worth the cruelty, the infidelity, the name-calling, the insults, the mood swings, all because I believed that since I had won him over in the first place, I just had to try a little bit harder for his affection. I knew the way he talked to me and the way he made me feel about myself weren't right. And yet, I always seemed to come back to it. Not just El Paso, but *this*, fighting myself to understand what was real, how I let it get to this point, and trying to convince myself that things would be good if I just worked a little harder.

I had suspicions he was not entirely committed to me, but I couldn't prove it. Whenever I brought my misgivings to his attention, he managed to convince me I was crazy, that my instincts were wrong, and I was just jealous. That was until I found naked pictures of Verna attached to his emails during one of my weekend visits.

I didn't confront him about the pictures. Not only would it be useless, but I strangely relished my discovery. It finally gave me something real, something *tangible*, to cling to so I could convince myself that I had to leave him. Those pictures gave me certainty. They gave me strength.

My body told its most convincing lie ever the night I found the pictures. I was affectionate, loving, and attentive. I offered him a drink, a snack, a hug each time I moved from room to room, gathering my things and packing them away for my flight home the next day. Trying not to seem too eager to leave, I moved slowly and cautiously. Starting an argument would devolve quickly into him criticizing and me pleading with him to see I wasn't fat or disgusting or stupid or worthless, as he had told me so many times before. No, I wanted that night to be calm and quiet so I wouldn't relapse into being desperate for him to keep me.

His suspicion came the following afternoon when he drove me to the airport. It was the first time I didn't cry over the thought of leaving him and returning to Ohio, even though the program made me feel worse about myself than he did. As much as I tried, I couldn't fake tears. I sat in the passenger seat of his black Viper, dry-eyed and silent as we crossed the New Mexico state line into Texas, the last time I would travel eastbound on I-10. Staring ahead, I wanted to remember the distant shacks positioned on the mountain, just on the other side of the river, but still Mexico, still a foreign country.

Raul's face was hidden under the reflection from his glasses.

"I'm going to miss you," I lied. But in the weeks ahead, it would become true. I would miss him and struggled with myself not to go back. Because I had given up so much to be with him, there was nothing left to fill his absence after moving on.

"I'll miss you, too, Tubby." *Tubby*. His nickname for me. A constant reminder that his idea of affection was to insult me. He hadn't called me by my real name in months.

I checked my watch as we approached the terminal. After nearly a year of traveling back and forth to visit him, I had experienced every travel delay and disruption imaginable. This time, though, the sky was clear, and I was nearly two hours early for my flight. For once, the weather was on my side.

Raul took my bag out of the trunk and set it on the ground, avoiding eye contact. He was angry again, quiet, shifty, and distant. Typically, I would start to panic and pester him with questions, trying to figure out what triggered his mood. It was always something I did; I just never knew what exactly.

"I'm sad to leave," I lied again, hoping to soften him up. I hadn't cried at all that morning and was worried he had caught on to my untruth. He knew exactly how to keep me clinging to him. By the time I leaned in to give him a hug, he barely put one arm around me.

"Goodbye, Tubby," he said with irritation in his voice.

I wanted to slap him for that infernal nickname. He had carried on some Internet romance with a woman I was always highly suspicious of, and I hated myself for not paying attention to my reservations even more than I hated him. Walking up to the ticket counter and pulling my duffle bag behind me, I felt duped and defeated. Another relationship failed, another promise broken. So I did what any self-respecting women who had no other idea about how to take control of her life would do: Paid ninety dollars I couldn't afford and upgraded my seat to first class.

El Paso is ugly. I studied the boxy city through the airplane window. This was my fifth trip flying out of that airport within one year, and its sparse brown, mute ugliness finally occurred to me. For the first time, I felt vindicated, that—literally—El Paso was beneath me.

At seventeen I boarded a plane for the first time to visit my grandparents in Florida. I was too old to pretend being able to see people in the cars below me and too old to wonder if they could see me. My younger siblings traveled with me, though, and they could imagine it, so I let them negotiate the window seat. When we started to taxi, I closed my eyes, breathed deeply through my nose, and tried not to throw up as we ascended into the air. It was during that trip I discovered motion sickness affects me beyond the backseat on my parents' station wagon. Flying out of El Paso nine years later, I didn't vomit but seethed. Outwardly I was calm, distant, self-assured. Inwardly, I was lost in obsessive thoughts, refusing to let go of those naked images of Verna, a woman with unmatchable exotic beauty and a sense of humor that even he could appreciate. I couldn't compete with her and shouldn't have to, either.

On the plane, the cabin darkened around me, and I looked out my window at a single pink streak across the blackening horizon. The shifting clouds flashed over it, and I caught my reflection in the window. I turned away, not wanting to be reminded of all the times I stared into a mirror for hours, smoothing my hair, studying my skin for blemishes, determined to see the flaws he could see and desperate to fix them. Raul reminded me all the time that he believed my tattoos and my upbringing made me trashy and worthless, and I had to spend more time on my appearance to overcome that.

I bit into a warm cashew and washed it down with a sip of chardonnay then reached up to turn on the light above me and sank back in my seat. First-class was full of perks, and I smirked inwardly at how easy it was to pretend. As a graduate assistant teaching one composition class a semester and making about $16,000 a year, I didn't belong in first class then or ever, but nobody around me had to know that. For a few hours I could pretend that my life was different, that I was deserving of more, of being treated well.

My self-efficacy was short-lived. I made it two weeks alone in my studio apartment in Ohio, only leaving to attend my classes or teach my students, before Raul was back in my life. There needed to be one final phone call, one last conversation that would leave me feeling everything that needed to be said, was said. The warm cashews and free chardonnay on the airplane couldn't repair the damage Raul had caused. Maybe I wanted his apology, his repentance, but I never got it. Instead, I got pulled back in, slowly, and assured that if we didn't have the distance between us, that we would survive. That geography was the problem, not him. I convinced myself that he wouldn't want me back if he didn't love me, if he didn't want to build a life with me.

After a year in Ohio, I caved to Raul's pressure and resigned from my teaching assistantship and dropped out of the doctorate program. I wasn't thriving the way I wanted to, and I felt competition instead of camaraderie with my classmates. Selling and giving away my belongings became my focus instead of studying, so I could drive myself and my cat back to New Mexico, back to Raul, to a place where there was no job, no family, and no opportunities, but I had him.

"What do you mean you're bringing your cat?" he asked me one evening after I complained about only being able to fit clothes and the feline into my small Toyota. "I can't have a cat here."

"We can get a different apartment." There was no way I could give up my cat.

"Why do I have to move?" he snarled. I felt that familiar pressure in my chest, causing my stomach to churn and nerves to ignite.

"What am I supposed to do?" I was accustomed to asking him for the answers. My body was rigid and tired, apologies already forming on my lips.

"Take it to a shelter."

A shelter. My cat, the one constant in my life for six years, and he wanted me to leave her at a shelter to be killed.

I felt an overwhelming sense of protectiveness and looked up at my cat lounging on the windowsill. After giving up all my belongings, I had to give up her now, too? I couldn't do it, *wouldn't* do it.

Conceding with Raul, I knew at that moment I wasn't going to move back to New Mexico. He had gotten away with treating me badly for so long that he must have thought his power extended to my pet, as well. But it didn't. I had already cancelled my lease and quit my job, so I couldn't stay in Ohio. Even though I was broke and should have felt lost and desperate, I didn't. Instead, I was hopeful. Ohio had become this place of digging my nails into a spoiled and damaged something. Breaking from Ohio would force me to break from the routine of attending classes, teaching classes, and fighting with Raul. Moving, this time, would actually mean moving on.

Chapter Four

It started with a phone call; at least I'm sure that's how Dan remembered it. For me, it actually started with the death rattle of my failed relationship with Raul, one that shredded my self-esteem like confetti strewn across a dance floor. I always idealized Dan as my first high school love. However, it was a love that never manifested into anything but a friendship in which he was kind to me even though he knew how much I pined for him. In the years that followed, at every relationship's end, I thought of Dan and looked back trying to identify why I was drawn to the wrong men.

After the breakup with Raul, I thought that maybe, just maybe, connecting with ghosts of love's past would give me some kind of closure, some kind of personal understanding to help me move forward. Starting with Dan was the logical choice. I sent him an email with my phone number, and he called a few days later.

That first conversation was no more than eleven minutes of polite exchanges, small talk disrupted by noticeable silences or interruptions to avoid the silences. I told him I was moving back to Michigan at the end of August. What I didn't tell him was that I had nowhere else to go, without a job or any prospects, and would be sleeping on an air mattress in my parents' basement until life stabilized, not knowing how long that could take. Despite how unimpressive I was, he still suggested we could have lunch or something and catch up. After hanging up the phone, I noticed a slight, but distinct layer of sweat around my hairline and warmth in my cheeks. I was twenty-six years old and just talking to that boy on the phone had me flustered. It was as though high school had never ended.

Just four weeks after that awkward and nervous re-introduction, he stood at the end of the driveway holding the passenger door of his car open.

"You look great," he said, and I knew he meant it. He stepped forward with arms outstretched and hugged me. I had waited more than a decade for him to respond to me that way. Perhaps this was my chance to get it right.

It had been almost ten years since we last saw each other. We were just teenagers then. He was a wrestler and on the football team, full of confidence and the kind of guy everyone wanted to be around. I was a dark and brooding introvert who edited the literary magazine, directed the school plays, wore over-sized clothes, and let my hair hang over my face if it happened to fall that way. During high school we had one date. He took me to the homecoming dance my junior year; I asked him, and he went because he was too nice to say no. I wore a purple satin dress that hung just above my knees. When he picked me up, he handed me a single rose instead of strapping a corsage to my wrist. It was the closest I had ever come to calling him my boyfriend. For me, that wasn't nearly close enough.

After graduation I cut ties with all things high school, including Dan. I heard brief stories about him throughout the years, but nothing substantial enough to think I knew anything about him as an adult. In many ways I hoped he knew just as little about me.

For my twenty-seventh birthday Dan and I made up our own bar crawl along the streets of downtown Ferndale. Ferndale was what Hamtramck hoped to become. Like Hamtramck, it was a city that bordered Detroit. At one time it was unsafe, barren, no drawing power. While I was away growing up and earning my degrees, Ferndale had grown, too. Young couples—straight and gay—bought houses, established businesses, and remade the community. The streets of Ferndale now looked like actual neighborhoods, where people sat on their front porch in the summer, and who shoveled each other's driveways after a heavy snowfall. Dan's parents had moved to Ferndale a few years after he graduated high school. Watching the city evolve in front of him inspired him to change Hamtramck in the same way.

The night of my birthday, I had the displeasure of making awkward small talk with his mom in their kitschy living room. It was like I was fifteen again with slightly better skin and much longer hair. But this time, instead of hoping her son would hold my hand or even kiss me at some point that night, I knew in a few hours we would be drunk and naked in her basement defiling the floral retro couch like we had done so many times already that summer. He was living with his parents, and I was living with mine. We were two teenagers in our late twenties without the modesty of our youth to hold us back.

The rare moments of affection came from me, after sex. They were subtle, but ever-present. He would lie on his stomach facing away from me, and I ran my fingertips up and down his back, alternating between a gentle, almost tickling touch and light massage.

"You're so giving," he said.

"Don't expect me to fall in love with you," I told him that night. "I'm not fifteen anymore." I smiled to make it seem like a joke, but it wasn't. Maybe I imagined it. Maybe I made it up. But for just a moment, a look of sadness—maybe disappointment, maybe hurt—flashed across his face.

Our affair carried on into the fall, after I found a job and finally got an apartment. With the change in seasons came a change in desire for each other. Our incompatibilities were gradually becoming more evident, and any ability to satisfy each other physically dwindled. One time when making out went on for just a little too long, and his moaning was just a little too distracting to be sexy, I could tell we were both about to lose our stamina. I had the window A/C unit on full blast and my iPod hooked into speakers next to the bed, hoping the downstairs neighbors couldn't hear every bump and creak of the mattress through the floorboards.

He let out a noise that could only be described as a frustrated growl, reached over my head, scrolled ahead to "Bohemian Rhapsody," and climbed on top of me, pumping away to the cadence of the music. His focus and rhythm told me I had until the end of the song to get my shit together or the opportunity of getting anything out of it would soon pass. I didn't make it. What I didn't know was that on the nights his phone went unanswered, he was spending time with someone else, someone new. It hadn't occurred to me that there could be the possibility of another for him, just as there was no possibility of another for me. But there was, there was.

Dan's voice muffled the backdrop of a dribbling basketball, sneakers squealing with each pivot and turn, and the dull roar of a cheering crowd when he looked over at me and said, "She spent the night last night."

Tracy. Her name had come up a lot lately. I didn't understand why. She wasn't pretty. Instead, she had the look of a woman who was never happy: unfocused and vacant eyes, and a mouth that turned downward at the corners when smiling. I knew from her online profile that she couldn't construct a complex sentence or spell a word with two or more syllables, and she abused the exclamation point.

"We didn't have sex," he said. He looked at me and then back at the court. "Not that I didn't want to."

My mind flashed to what that scenario must have looked like. He had just moved into a house in Hamtramck, a working-class town that overlapped Detroit. Once a thriving neighborhood of Polish immigrants employed by the auto industry, Hamtramck had come undone, much like other cities feeling the consequences of a failed economy—poverty, abandoned homes, drugs, vandalism. Yet there was a growing trend among up and coming twenty-somethings to move into those neighborhoods, work diligently to improve their homes, and consequently, the city, just like they had done in Ferndale decades before.

I knew that was Dan's motivation for moving there. However, it didn't change the fact that for the moment his bed was a mattress on the hardwood floor, the same bed Tracy shared with him. What possible romance or seduction could occur in a house with barely any furniture, heat that worked only sometimes, and bars on the windows? Then again, what she found appealing about his house likely mirrored what he found appealing about her, and all I knew was I couldn't understand any of it.

The basketball game was nearly over with our team losing, but neither one of us were paying attention. I stared into my cup and listened to him; it was my third beer on an empty stomach, and felt it.

"Let's go," I said. "If we leave now, we can beat the traffic."

Climbing into the car, I positioned my high-heeled, boot-clad feet over the pedals. I had no business driving, especially not twenty minutes on the freeway in the dark, but I put the key in the ignition and started the engine anyway. At that moment, I didn't think about legality or consequences. I just wanted to be able to have a conversation without looking at him, and driving was the only way I could do that. To stay alert, I rolled down the window before we got on the freeway. He was quiet in the seat next to me, and I tried not to appear mad. After all, I was supposed to be emotionally detached. That had been our agreement.

The wind hummed throughout the car. He put the window down halfway, sat back in the seat, and then put the window back up. I tried not to smirk at his discomfort.

"You need to figure out what you want," I finally said. "She probably senses that you can't commit."

He looked at me with an expression of surprise as if he had forgotten what we were talking about.

"I want to do the right thing."

I clutched the steering wheel tighter and focused on the road. Only ten more minutes until my exit. Relaxing a little because we were so close to home, I breathed in deeply and glanced over at Dan. He wasn't looking at me.

The right thing. I knew what that meant; the situation wasn't going to work out in my favor.

"Figure out what you want first, and then make your decision. Someone is always going to get hurt. That's the risk you take." I paused to change lanes as the exit approached. "If it's me that you hurt in the process, I promise I will get over it."

He listened to me, nodding his head. I parked on the street in front of a house where I rented the upstairs apartment. Before I even turned off the ignition he said, "Am I using you if I'm with you when I can't be with her?"

Without an answer, I climbed out of my car and walked toward the house. I didn't look back, but I knew he was right behind me. The conversation wasn't over.

We didn't speak while we climbed the stairs together or while I struggled with a sticky key in the deadbolt. He stayed silent while I took two beers from the fridge and popped the caps directly into the trashcan. We stood on my porch, a beer bottle rested on the railing next to me, the souvenir cup from the game already rinsed and placed in the dishwasher.

"You're extraordinary," he said to me. I didn't know why we were outside, and more importantly, why I wasn't wearing a jacket on an October evening. Even though I shivered, I didn't suggest we go inside, didn't even look at him. His words would have been a comfort if they had been said in a different context. How do you respond when someone ruins a great compliment by leaving you?

"Are you mad?" he asked. "You're quiet."

My beer bottle was empty. I had half a mind to let it slip out of my hand and fall to the ground two stories below the balcony. "No. I'm not mad. I'm just taking it all in."

He shook his head and looked away. "I shouldn't have touched you."

Regret hung in the air between us.

The next morning, I rolled over to face him; he was already awake and waiting for me. He put his arm out, and I settled in next to him, resting my head on his shoulder.

"Is this the end?" I asked.

"Yeah."

I didn't pull away. Instead, I said, "You may not know what it is that you want, but at least you know now what you don't want."

"You told me you can't love me," he said. He had clung to that, unable to realize the lie.

"I know."

It wasn't safe to let my guard down, not after what I had gone through with Raul. I didn't let on that I was upset, so I upheld my story that for us, it was casual. For us it was transitory. That for me, it was unemotional and didn't have anything to do with love.

I didn't cry. But then he grabbed me and kissed me, hard; his lips square against mine, his hands around my elbows pulling me into him. My breath caught the moan in my throat, turned it to a gasp, and the rush of emotion brought the tears. *Dammit.*

Yet, there was no sobbing, no begging him to reconsider. There was no ridiculous over-pouring of emotions or confession of hidden love. Instead I pulled away, smiled, wiped the tears from my face, and offered to take him home. In the car, we drove through tunnels of trees that had all turned to yellow, orange, and red. Summer was over.

A year after that final night together, I found myself back at that moment, standing in my kitchen, wondering how it was so easy for yet another man in my life to want nothing from me but half-drunk sex on his terms.

"It was my way of convincing myself that it was okay, even though it wasn't," Dan said to me while we sat on a patio outside a coffee shop in Hamtramck, the tail end of summer making it just warm enough to break a sweat, the sun too bright for September.

We hid our eyes behind sunglasses; I hid my shame behind a smile.

I forced him to tell me what I meant to him when we were together.

"I'm not trying to make you feel guilty," I said. "But I need to find a way to make sense of all this."

He was quiet for a while, not wanting to tell me the truth. I pushed my sunglasses up on top of my head, leaned in, and waited.

"It was easier for me that way," he said. "I told myself that I gave you an out by letting you know I wasn't looking for anything serious. I didn't have to feel guilty then."

I leaned back in the chair and crossed my arms to settle in for what was coming.

"This guy," he paused, trying to remember a name, but then realized the name didn't matter. "This guy just wants to have some fun. And he's getting what he wants without having to give you anything."

"Is that why you did it?" It was a hard question, but I didn't care.

"I got what I wanted, but I couldn't give you what you needed," he said. "Tracy." It was the first time he said her name unprovoked. "Tracy didn't need anything from me. It was easy."

I leaned into my folded hands with elbows resting on the arms of the plastic chair. That moment, I didn't feel much of anything. Not fully understanding his words, I was still able to empathize with his position.

He told me he was sorry if he hurt me, that I deserved something—some*one*—better. I appreciated his kindness and told him so. When our conversation ended, I got back into my car and got lost leaving Hamtramck. I drove up and down streets where the houses were much too close together, the yards much too small, the parking much too limited for my taste. When I found my way back to the freeway, I lowered the visor to keep the sun out of my eyes and drove home. I had nowhere else to go.

We had jumped too fast. Raul couldn't fix my marriage, and a love affair with Dan couldn't fix Raul. They were easy to blame for the dissolution of whatever it was that I had with them, but the only constant in each situation was me. I couldn't give myself to a man with hope that he would give me a commitment in return. It was wishful thinking, a barrier to critical analysis that I taught the students in college composition classes, so why couldn't I recognize it in my own decisions?

"It was logical inconsistency," I would tell them, "to draw conclusions based on limited information. Don't let your emotions interfere with your ability to reason in argumentation."

I couldn't let my emotions and hopes for a companion interfere anymore, either. It wasn't reasonable for me to expect a man who wanted nothing from me to give me anything I needed. I would have to set that standard for myself.

Chapter Five

Dave was twenty minutes late for our first date, looking annoyed but not at all apologetic. He sat across from me at the high-top pub table, and when the waitress came to take our drink order he asked, "Do you want to do a shot?"

Although I had been of legal drinking age for more than six years, I had never actually ordered a shot at a bar, and it especially hadn't occurred to me to do so during dinner. But his question was serious and the offer legitimate, so I conceded. I ordered straight tequila because I couldn't think of anything else and they were both staring at me, waiting for an answer.

"With training wheels," he told the waitress.

I nodded, though didn't know it meant with salt and a lime chaser until the waitress set the extras on the table in front of me.

Dave and I met two weeks prior. Ian was in town for his sister's wedding and gathered his friends together before the nuptials so he could spend time with everyone at once. I hadn't seen Ian since my trip to Las Vegas and knew there would be a few old high school classmates there as well. The only thing in my way was Raul. It wasn't until I left Ohio, and actually moved to Michigan instead of back to New Mexico, that he realized the relationship was truly over.

During the weeks I had lived in my parents' basement while searching for a job and a place to live, Raul called me daily, addressed me as "Beautiful," and eventually started crying and expressing his regret for taking me for granted, for not appreciating me when he had the chance I finally had what I always desired: his unrelenting affection, and I wanted nothing to do with it.

Yet, I wasn't quite able to break free from him. His compliments and attention were flattering, and it was a nice escape from reality to let him coo at me while I fired off my resume for the countless time. It took more than a hundred applications to receive an interview, and during that time of uncertainty, Raul was a constant source of familiarity and reassurance. Even though he feigned support for my pursuits, I could tell he wanted my professional endeavors in Michigan to fail so I might return to New Mexico to be with him. I worked diligently to make sure that didn't happen, all the while smiling along with his short-lived kindness.

Soon after I moved into my apartment and Dan moved on to Tracy, I gave in to Raul's insistence on visiting me in Michigan. It was October, and the crisp air and changing leaves were seasonal pleasures that he had never experienced living his whole life in the desert. Although I didn't love him anymore, I welcomed his company. My fling with Dan had been fleeting, and I missed having some kind of companionship. I hadn't made many friends at that point, and I often felt lonely on the weekends. Having a friend in town, even if it was Raul, would give me a break from that loneliness.

Ian's get-together was the same day Raul arrived. I picked him up from the airport and drove him around the city without mentioning the party. When we got to the apartment, he wanted to lie on the bed together, just like those early days when we would spend our time together lounging and looking up and away and not at each other. After a few minutes, I weaseled away from him and went to the closet. Speaking into my clothes, I told him about going out that night.

"Do you want to come with me?"

He conceded. "I'm not going to hang out here by myself."

I was surprised by his response because he had never gone anywhere with me when we were together in Las Cruces. Raul was trying to present himself as a changed man, though I suspected that once he got comfortable again and felt secure, he would revert back to his old self. He hadn't really changed; he was only acting differently, and the act—I knew—was temporary.

Ian greeted me at the door just as we arrived, looking at Raul guardedly. He knew all about him. I could tell he was concerned but was still friendly and welcoming, still Ian. A tall man in a striped button-down shirt and jeans approached us, and Ian introduced him as Dave, someone who went to the same college as we did.

We chatted for a minute before Raul went to the front to get me a drink. I turned to Ian quickly and said, "We're not back together, okay? He insisted on visiting, and I finally gave in."

"I was wondering," Ian said. "But I wasn't going to say anything."

"I know. That's why I thought I should just clear the air."

As the night passed, Ian circulated from group to group, mingling and laughing with friends in a way that only Ian could do. He had the ability to make the person he was talking to feel like the most important person in the room, and the conversation would be so fulfilling that it wouldn't seem rude when he moved on to talk to someone else.

Dave mingled with others, too, but he kept coming back to me, just enough to be friendly but not overbearing. Raul stood to the side and pretended to watch the football game on the television. I knew better; he hated football, but he had no idea how to act or what to say even when I tried to bring him into the conversation.

That night, when I was driving us back to the apartment, my cell phone rang. The number was Ian's, but the voice wasn't.

"Hi Melissa, it's Dave. That guy you just met? I'm calling from Ian's phone."

Raul sat in the passenger seat next to me, straining to listen in on the conversation.

Dave asked if I might want to hang out sometime, as he put it, and if so, he could get my number from Ian.

Feeling tense, I gave one-word responses to avoid raising suspicion and quickly hung up the phone. Raul grilled me with questions anyway, and I answered him honestly. After all, I owed him nothing and had been trying to move on.

When Dave called Monday night and invited me out, I agreed to join him for dinner, even knowing very little about him. While we talked, Dave sat sideways in his seat, body facing away from me. He smoked, holding the cigarette at his side and exhaling into the air above him. I felt myself getting drunk, and with that, more open and talkative.

He asked me about past relationships. I didn't share too many details of my history aside from having married young and divorced young because other than that five-year relationship, there wasn't much to share.

"But I have dated enough to have a set of standards," I said. "I used to be more accepting, more open-minded. But now I have my deal breakers." He didn't know that those deal breakers had not been long-standing, but were instead the result of the promise made to myself to not fall into the same patterns as with previous men in my life.

He put his beer down and leaned in.

"Let's hear them."

I sat back. "My deal breakers?"

"Well, yeah." He smiled a little and crushed his cigarette out in the tray in front of him. "I want to know what kind of chance I have."

"Okay." My shoulders shifted as I relaxed against the stiff wooden back of the chair. Until he asked, it hadn't occurred to me to have an actual list. I ticked the traits off on the tips of my fingers, trying to read some kind of reaction as the list got longer and longer.

"No kids. No drugs. Done with school. Financially stable and smart about money. Doesn't live with his parents, though he needs to have a good relationship with them. Doesn't brood, pout, or yell. Doesn't cheat, doesn't lie, and doesn't lie about cheating. Isn't lazy and will be nice to my cat. Isn't rude to wait staff. Doesn't spend all his free time playing video games. Doesn't break promises. Finally, doesn't smoke."

He nodded along. "Aside from the smoking, I think I'm still good." He chuckled, as if proud of himself.

I ran the tip of my tongue across my front teeth. "But smoking is a big one."

"I eat a lot of mints. Does that help? I'm probably more addicted to mints than I am to cigarettes."

Shaking my head, already I wondered if this was going anywhere. I questioned my attraction to him and if he could even live up to my expectations.

"And he has to give me the stomach-flip. No stomach flip, and it just won't work."

"The what?"

Before I had a chance to answer, the waitress came over and asked if we wanted to order anything else. I shook my head before Dave had a chance to offer me another shot.

"Here's the deal," he said. "When the bill comes, I'm paying. I don't want to play that reaching-for-your-wallet game, you know?"

Dave signed the bill, and his handwriting was like a child's with all capitals, the rounded letters exaggerated, the pointed edges sharp.

He always paid back then.

I would pay later.

Dave finished his pint, slammed the glass down, leaned in and tapped the table with his index finger. "I want to take you to my favorite bar," he said. "It's dark, it's dirty, and it's cash only. And you might get hepatitis if you sit on the toilet seat, so you should probably pee before we leave."

I raised my eyebrows. He was forward in a way that I wasn't accustomed to. It made me more curious about him, so I agreed to the rendezvous. It was November, and I shivered in my thin jacket when we stepped outside. As we walked quickly to his car, he reached back and took my hand in his. His gait was heavy; he dragged his left leg slightly behind his right. My footsteps were light and distinctive as the heels of my shoes clicked along the asphalt.

When we arrived, I lingered for a moment outside the door, experiencing a minor case of threshold resistance. He pulled me in by the hand, and I tried to not make eye contact with any of the patrons clad in leather and chains or flannel shirts and work boots. He walked up to the bar and ordered two shots. When the bartender turned to make our drinks, Dave pulled me into him, bent me over and kissed me hard square on the mouth, the pressure parting my lips to accept his tongue. Stomach flips abounded.

*

It was in the back of a jazz club during our visit to Chicago that Dave confessed his gambling problem. He had left Las Vegas and returned to Michigan just narrowly avoiding jail time for taking out two markers at the Palms Casino he couldn't repay. In Clark County, such an act is equivalent to writing bad checks which is classified as a felony.

We sat in the club with music and smoke around us. Dave was too drunk to drive, and I was too drunk to judge, so I let the information blanket me. I didn't fully understand that his term, "compulsive gambler," meant "gambling addict," not until later, anyway.

"I've been to therapy," he said. "I'm recovered." The experience left him with a less-than stellar credit rating, but he had stopped gambling. I believed him because he gave me no reason not to.

Four months later, I could sense something had changed. The seemingly laid-back and jovial guy was short with me. Distant. Dave appeared overwhelmed and worn out. He would lose track of time and arrive two or three hours late, or sometimes not at all. I would wonder, and wait, and give him the benefit of the doubt because there was always an explanation, always an excuse.

That was until he confessed he had been sneaking off to Detroit casinos and losing his time and money at the poker tables. He stood in front of me and waited for a response while I sat on the edge of my bed and stared at the floor, letting the tension build in the room around us.

I didn't know what to say to him. Dave had lied. He told me he didn't gamble anymore, and then he went right ahead and did it. An apology wouldn't matter, as apologies aren't true until behaviors actually change.

Thinking of my ex-husband, of Raul, even of Dan, I wondered if I had found the same kind of man but in different packaging. I was angry, yes, but at whom? Ultimately, I felt Dave deserved another chance. My heart was a forgiving one; his was cunning and accepting of forgiveness.

So I gave him an ultimatum: if he gambled again, we were through. I couldn't be in a relationship where I was constantly suspicious of his whereabouts and his truth. He understood and promised—once again—that he was done, his face and demeanor agreeing with his words so much that I couldn't help but to believe him.

Again.

When I discovered he played online poker while I was out of town, using my computer to bet—and lose—more than six hundred dollars, I was once again confronted with Dave's unrelenting demons. By that time we had been dating nearly two years and living together for a few months, our lives so tightly intertwined that I was scared of what it meant for me to make good on my provocation to end the relationship.

I knew in that moment our long-term plans were over; I refused to set myself up for another divorce. But I wasn't ready to untangle myself from him, not just yet. I believed I was on the verge of a promotion at work and would have an easier time living on my own once that happened. Dave was covering half the bills, and it enabled me to save money, to set myself up for the opportunity to be on my own again. It would take time, though, so I stored away the poker game discovery and waited for when I would be ready to use it.

*

Dave slept a lot. He woke up in the morning just as I was leaving for work, and I would often find him dozing on the couch when I got home from teaching my evening classes. I would find his dirty dishes in the sink, the carpet not vacuumed, his clothes still strewn about the bedroom from the day before.

We had a chore chart to share household tasks, but he rarely completed the ones on his list. He was full of excuses that he needed to concentrate on his career, as he had recently taken a job as a financial planner, a position that paid on commission only. If he didn't convince people to purchase life insurance, roll over their 401ks, or invest in Roth IRAs, he didn't earn a paycheck. Nothing. He was always chasing money, as if he were back at the poker table, smoking his cigarettes and drinking nothing but Red Bull for days.

I sat at my desk grading final papers for an online summer class I taught when I turned to find Dave standing quietly in the doorway. He fidgeted, his posture mimicking his body language the night he admitted to gambling, that night so early in the relationship that I almost broke up with him.

He looked at the floor, then at me, and when I pulled my eyes away from the computer screen, he said, "I can't pay my half of the rent for August."

Dave was broke.

His decision to wait until three days before the rent was due to tell me was a deliberate one; all the while I lived my life and spent my money as if I didn't have to pay for both of us. He had me cornered. If I wanted to keep our apartment—and I did—I would have to cover his share. And he knew that. There was so much I wanted to say. But my silence was enough. I didn't need words to make my point.

"It's just this month," he said quickly. "I have some really good potential business lined up. I just have to close a few deals, and I'll be back on track. I know it will get better."

Every night after that I would hear different versions of the same story—he got a new lead, had a meeting with a new customer, established a rapport, was about to close a big deal, he just knew it, he could *feel* it. Every month he was closer to securing a sizable account, I just had to be a little more patient, a little more understanding, and just have a little more faith in him.

It was nearly another year before he would be able to pay again. Each month it was the same story, the same empty promises. But I believed them. I believed him, knowing that when this big deal came, I would be able to reclaim all the money I had spent keeping us sheltered and fed. Once that deal came, then I could leave. Then I would be ready.

*

When Dave called me at work on an early Tuesday afternoon, I could tell from his voice that it was a conversation I needed to have with my door closed. I shooed some lingering students out of my office and sat down at my desk.

"I don't know how to tell you this," he said. He was quiet for a long time, and I could hear the television on in the background even though it was the middle of the afternoon. *Why wasn't he at work?*

"You know I went to the doctor today right?"

"Yeah," I said, even though I didn't remember. Tired of the empty promises, I didn't pay much attention to anything he said anymore.

"Well," he said. "I have an STD."

I pressed the phone harder to my ear, certain I hadn't heard him right. So many moments in my life I had imagined a phone call like this. I still wasn't prepared.

"What? How?" As if I didn't know. Our money problems had caused so much friction between us that it had been four—maybe five, six?—months since we'd had sex. It was hard to keep track when I was living the same day over and over while he made the same assurances over and over, and I had learned to not count on them.

Sitting in my office, I was calm, patient, but distant. I thought briefly of our first date when he warned me about contracting hepatitis from the toilet seat, and shook my head at the irony. Both times I had avoided infection.

"What do you have?" Terms from my high school health class flashed through my mind: syphilis, gonorrhea, chlamydia, crabs.

"Genital warts," he said. "You know, HPV?"

It took a long pause on the phone for me to piece it all together. He was infected. *Fear.* He obviously didn't get it from me. *Relief.* He had to get it from somewhere. *Suspicion.* I worked late two nights a week, my schedule well-known and predictable. *Anger.* I also often visited my parents in Chicago on weekends. *Rage.* And then, a sudden memory of his phone ringing at 2:30 in the morning early in our relationship, and his dismissive laughter that he forgot to notify his booty calls he was now in a relationship. *Fury.* The odds had been stacked against him, against us, from the beginning.

Dave was talking fast. "The doctor said it's common; it's not a big deal. He just burned them off, and when I go back he'll check for more, and burn those off, too. It's nothing to freak out about, It's—"

I stopped listening. The tone and pace of his voice were the same as those many conversations when he insisted and eventually convinced me the next big deal was within reach. He didn't convince me anymore. There was no more convincing me of anything.

Later that night I sat at the kitchen table, my head in my hands, and said, "I'm so tired of paying for your mistakes. So, so tired." The gambling, the financial strain, and now—though he denied it—the cheating. Our relationship had no truth. My world cracked inside of me, and I was left without answers, without decisions, and even without questions, only an absolution: He wasn't someone who I could build a future with. Though I had known it, I was finally prepared to act on it.

When I told Dave his inability and refusal to contribute to the relationship—financially or otherwise—had brought me to the conclusion he needed to move out, he was armed with responses, fully prepared to argue with me as if he had planned the conversation all along.

"I don't want to break up," he started.

I put my hand up. "I know about the online poker game." The smoking gun.

He opened his mouth. Closed it. Shook his head. Snickered. *Smiled.* Opened his mouth again. Closed it. Finally, all he could say was, "I can't believe you kept quiet about it for this long."

When he asked to meet me for dinner two days later and suggested couple's counseling, I told him I was willing to consider it, but he needed to move out anyway.

"I need to know that you can make it on your own," I said. "I need to know that you're with me for us, not because it's convenient."

"If I move out," he said. "Then we're done."

We sat on a bench along the downtown sidewalk watching passers-by enjoy the beginnings of summer. *Then we're done.* He gave me an ultimatum, his plan deliberate and pre-meditated. Dave didn't want to fix the relationship. He just didn't want to move out, to have to pay his own way for the first time in nearly a year.

"Then I guess we're done," I said. "You didn't do your part to keep us together. I'm not doing my part now." I quivered under the weight of the words, shoulders shaking, while I sat on that bench. It was both terrifying and exhilarating to be so forthcoming with him, to be the one to make the right decision. Finally.

For thirty days, Dave insisted he couldn't find a decent apartment.

Everything he found was too expensive, in the wrong neighborhood, too far from work, too small.

I didn't argue with him. Instead, I took all of his suits out of my closet, threw them down the stairs, and screamed, "Why can't you see that I don't want you here?"

Within a week, he found an apartment.

Within two, he was gone.

Chapter Six

One of the first things I did after Dave moved out was convert his office into a guest bedroom. I ripped out the stained and dirty carpet, repainted the forest green walls a calming blue, and bought a futon and dresser to give it some semblance of an inviting place to rest.

But it wasn't enough. I wanted to rejuvenate my home, to rid it of both the things he loved and those he complained about because I needed to eradicate memories of him. Although I had done the bulk of the labor when it came to working on the house after I bought it, Dave was not without his opinions. His preference for dark, muddy colors and television-centric layouts was still evident throughout most of the space.

Each morning, I rolled onto my back and studied the room around me. He had picked the gray paint color for the bedroom walls, but it was something I could live with. The dark bedding and the cluttered furniture, though, had to go. The bed could be rotated to rest up against a different wall, so when I propped myself up to read, I wasn't pressing my back against the window. It was time to make the room comfortable for me, to use it in the way I wanted. I didn't need anyone's permission or approval anymore. It didn't matter that the ceiling was too low or the room didn't have dark enough curtains to keep out the morning sun. If it worked for me, then it worked.

All the small decorative changes didn't compare to the resentment I had toward the master bathroom, a long and narrow room with brown everything: linoleum, cabinetry, paint colors. There had been water damage at one point from a leaking faucet connector, and the base of the vanity was a mess of molded and shredded wood as the water had seeped through it and onto the floor, curling some tiles and rippling others. Whoever had installed the fixtures had gotten carried away with a caulk gun as well, leaving thick, heavy globs of the stuff around the base of the toilet, bathtub, and shower wall.

I stared into that bathroom from my bed, and every morning wished away the brown, the dirt, the carelessness, the damage. The mirror was always dotted with water spots and toothpaste, a constant argument between Dave and I, where he would blame the mess on being too tall and the counter being too short, and I would blame him for being thoughtless and lazy. That mirror was never clean; no matter how many times I wiped it down, clearing the drips and the smudges. He also had the habit of shaking out his hands over the sink after he washed them, a habit that would send water drops all over the counter, water drops he never cleaned up after drying his hands. These were the kind of reminders I wanted to be rid of, the kind of memories I didn't want to hit me unexpectedly while I stood in front of the mirror each morning brushing my own teeth, taking care to spit toothpaste into the sink and nowhere else.

I decided to do something I never imagined I could do on my own: I was going to remodel my master bathroom. The task would involve taking out all the hated stuff and replacing it with stuff that I would not hate. I was lucky enough to have a nice soaker with jets, so it wouldn't be necessary for me to try and replace a bathtub. Everything else, though, either needed a facelift or replacing.

Dave's enthusiasm for these kinds of projects waned soon after we moved into the house. He did his part to help with the first phase of kitchen updates and even framed out a place to add a door leading to the upstairs bedroom so there would be more than a set of stairs separating us from the rest of the house. The other projects, though, those were always left up to me. In contrast, when John and I were married, there was very little that I was trusted to do myself. Every furniture purchase, every painted wall, every picture hung always happened under his supervision. While Dave didn't have much regard for how the house looked, John was too concerned, too controlling, too dictatorial about everything. I wasn't sure which I preferred more.

The large bathroom mirror was nothing more than a thin sheet of reflective glass screwed into the wall at each of the four corners. The screws came out with ease, but as I tried to pull the mirror away from the wall, it stuck to an old layer of paint, and broke into jagged pieces, one of which sliced deep into the index finger on my left hand. I barely noticed the cut, choosing instead to wrap a paper towel around my finger and keep going, even when the blood oozed through and dripped onto the tile.

After ripping out the beige cultured marble sink-top, the vanity beneath it fell apart so easily I was surprised it had remained intact for so long. As I stretched on tip-toes to finish the wiring for the new light fixture, my knees wobbled, gave out, and I stumbled backward, landing butt-first in the bathtub, my legs draped over the edge. I gave an exhale of growling frustration and sat for a minute, knees up to my chest, feet suspended in the air on the other side of the tub.

All of my focus the past three days had been on the bathroom, a project I could obsess over that would actually have a positive outcome. With so much time spent on demolition, I didn't make time for meals. The dizziness and wobbling knees reminded me I couldn't keep up the same efforts without eating. I thought to order pizza—always an easy option—and was reminded of the first day in my apartment when I moved back to Michigan, back when Raul was trying to keep my attention. He went online and ordered pizza for me and had it delivered to my door. I didn't have cash for a tip, and there was no way to add it to the order, so I had to send the delivery man away without compensation for his troubles. He had smiled and assured me it was okay, that I would "get him next time," but I never felt more embarrassed than I did watching that man descend the rickety wooden staircase, his hands and pockets empty.

The beige toilet was the next to go, so I could scrape the peeling tiles off the subfloor. They left behind a sticky, dirty layer of glue that suctioned to my knees as I hovered over the drain hole, poking at the broken flange and trying to figure out how to replace it. A quick skimming of research provided universal guidance: it must be chiseled out. The guidance, though, came with a consistent warning: Do not break the drain pipe.

It was a Saturday. A broken drain pipe would mean a bathroom out of commission for an indeterminate amount of time, depending on the cost and availability of a plumber. More than the inconvenience of it all, though, I was concerned the failed attempt to remove the flange on my own would mean literally paying for a mistake, a mistake I could have avoided if I had only been more cautious. But calling a plumber to do this part for me came with its own type of admittance and forced me to question the commitment I had made to this project and the confidence I could do it myself.

I wanted—*needed*—something that was my own, that I had started and finished without the help of anyone, without relying on a man to offer his opinion and expertise. Like so many decisions before this one, it all came down to a realistic understanding of my competence and confidence, and the ability to make a sound and rational judgment. I had failed at this decision-making ability when it came to relationships. Was removing a toilet so different?

After reading tutorials and reviewing step-by-step diagrams, I watched video after video of men in hats and overalls removing broken flanges. Finally, my impatience and stubbornness got the better of me, and I gathered all the tools I could possibly imagine needing and spread them out on the floor. Fitting a saw into the pipe opening presented itself as the first challenge until I tried the jigsaw and had just enough space and control to cut five or six notches in the plastic, a quarter of an inch apart, careful not to go too deep. I wrapped my fingers around a chisel, one of a set of three Dave insisted I buy when I asked him to hang a door in the space leading to the upstairs bedroom. The chisels seemed like a ridiculous and unnecessary purchase at the time, one that caused me to make a scene at the checkout counter the next time we went shopping; I refused to pay for all the things he dropped into the cart without thought.

In the bathroom, though, the chisel felt like a life force. I placed the end against the outside of the etched plastic, grabbed a hammer, and gently tap, tap, tapped on the butt end, my hands shaking.

Don't break, don't break, don't break, I pleaded, focused and anxious, wondering why there was so much doubt surrounding me—a woman— attempting to remodel a bathroom. *Maybe I should call someone; maybe I should have asked for help; maybe I am crazy; even if I get this toilet installed, maybe it will flood into the ceiling below until finally the water soaks into everything and the second floor collapses into the first, and I'm suddenly living in a one-story ranch instead of a two-story bungalow—*

The flange broke clear from the drain pipe in one solid piece in my hand. I scrambled backward, stood up, and yelled, "I did it! I did it!" then looked around and remembered I was alone. Not even the cat lifted her head up from the warmth of the bed to celebrate my triumph.

"And, nobody saw it," I sighed. It was a short-lived victory. But it was my own.

*

My sister called me, exasperated and shaken, on a rainy afternoon. She lived with her boyfriend in a house that was in the process of going into foreclosure. Although she had left him once for nearly a year— living in an ant-infested one-bedroom apartment with her daughter and working long hours—it wasn't enough. She couldn't make ends meet and couldn't stand to be alone. Before long, she moved in with him again, into the house his parents had walked away from, not caring her shelter would soon expire.

"Can you come get me?" Mary Beth pleaded into the phone. She always had a proclivity for drama, a type of over-acting that my parents credited to her being the middle child, so I didn't stop scanning my emails even when I heard desperation in her voice. There was always desperation in her voice, always some impossible struggle to face.

After a moment, I started to listen and learned in the midst of an argument, her boyfriend had picked up her flat screen television and thrown it across the room at her. When she ducked out the way, he became more furious and started throwing everything: the DVD player, the Wii, a stereo, picture frames, all smashing into the wall while their daughter watched from her bedroom doorway, screaming along with my sister, begging him to stop. I knew all about men who threw things and the rage that fueled their velocity. Raul liked to throw things, too.

"Yes, I can," I said. "I'll be there soon."

I parked my car in front of the house and climbed out slowly, not knowing what to expect. The grass was soggy beneath my feet as I walked across the yard toward the open front door, hearing no sound from within. Halfway across the lawn I paused to get my quickening breath under control. Water seeped into my shoes, and I pulled my cardigan tighter around me to ward off a chill. I wiped away the rain rolling down my temples, took a deep breath, and stepped toward the porch.

The door opened and my niece ran to me with her arms outstretched. Filled with relief, I picked her up, her little arms warm against my cold, wet cheek.

"I yelled at my dad," she whispered in my ear. "I told him I was going to your house." She pulled back and looked to my face for approval.

"Are you hurt?"

She shook her head and wriggled for me to put her down.

"Stay on the porch and out of the rain," I said. "Don't go back inside."

Moments later my sister stepped outside and looked in my direction. Not so much at me, but at the street behind me that would lead her, us, out of the neighborhood. She wasn't crying but looked as though she had been. I was surprised by how skinny she was, how skinny she had become. Her long hair was pulled back, but strands had fallen out of the rubber band and were hanging loose around her face.

"He said you can't come in." *William*. Her boyfriend. Keeping me outside and in the rain was his way of reminding my sister, and me, that he was the one in charge. He was the one in control.

I didn't protest because I knew how quickly his temper would escalate. Instead, Mary Beth passed boxes to me out the front door, and I piled them into my car and her minivan. She and William were still fighting. I could hear them, though their voices were chopped by the opening and closing of screen doors. Madison sat on the covered front porch and stayed there, just like I told her, sheltered from the rain.

William came outside and I stiffened. Rage was printed all over his face, and his eyes were dark and darting around until they settled on my niece. I had managed to keep her outside for an hour, and as long as she was in sight, I knew she was safe.

Holding her in my arms, I turned away from him. "Leave her alone. I don't trust you." She clung to me and wouldn't look at her father as I murmured reassurances into her ear.

He stared me down. I braced myself for a shove or a punch. Instead, he turned and went back into the house; though within minutes I could hear my sister screaming. She came out onto the porch just as I got to the door.

"He won't let me take Madison." She put both palms to her temples, fingers spread wide.

By taking my niece from him for a moment, he was going to take her from my sister for the night—or longer—just to remind us both he had the power.

I felt that same churning in my stomach when giving in to Raul's demands just to avoid an argument.

"She can't stay here," I said to Mary Beth. "You don't know what he'll do to her."

"She'll be fine." My sister was scared, but her words didn't reflect it. Even in the process of leaving him, she was still convinced William subscribed to some kind of moral code, that he wasn't a man-shaped monster. I wasn't so convinced.

He came outside with court paperwork in his hands and waved it at me, a demonic smile on his face. I approached him and stood on solid legs, legs Raul had once measured the circumference of as evidence that I needed to lose weight. My sister, waifish and shaken, stood behind me with her arms crossed.

"You're not taking my daughter." He leaned over me from the top of the porch, his narrow-set, beady eyes darkening. "If you do, it's kidnapping."

He had what the courts called the right of first refusal. He could, at any time and for any reason, refuse a caretaker for my niece, even if that caretaker was family, and at that moment, especially if that caretaker was me. Legally there was nothing I could do, and he knew it.

"She's terrified of you," I said, calling his fathering abilities into question, knowing it would anger him. I was stalling, trying to think of a way to get us all out of there.

"Do you really think I would hurt my own daughter?" He narrowed his eyes at me. "You have no right to talk to me like that. This is my house."

"You let her go," I said. "Or I'm calling the police."

He laughed. Right in my face. My sister shifted from one foot to the other, visibly nervous.

"Go ahead. They were already here, and they left. You're just wasting your time." He stood up straight. "I'll make sure they know that if you keep running your mouth, I won't hesitate to put you in your place."

For a moment, I tried to think of a way to make him hit me. His temper was bubbling just beneath the surface, and I knew if I could just get him to lose control, then I could press charges. But it wouldn't be enough. Even if I could get him arrested for the night, he would be out the next and ready to retaliate. I looked over at my niece. If I didn't get his permission to take her for the night, who knew when I would see her next?

Getting him to hit me wasn't a long-term solution. In so many ways he was Raul, and I knew it wasn't possible to outwit him with words or antagonize him to violence. I knew the way to calm down someone like William was to appear to give in, to lose.

So, I exhaled, softened my face, and looked directly at him. I forced an apologetic smile.

"I'm sorry." My voice cracked, and I even managed to push a few tears into my eyes. "I know you would never hurt her. I know you're a good dad. But imagine if you were me, and you came into this situation when I did. Wouldn't your greatest concern be for the child? I don't know what else to do. I'm just here to help my sister." I turned and looked at her, then back at him. "Because she asked me to."

On the corner of the porch my niece sat with her legs crossed. She smeared dirt from a spilled flower pot, muddying her clothes and shoes in the process. It didn't seem to matter to anyone but me that she was there witnessing the power play in her front yard.

"You're right. You're totally right. I'm sorry," I said again. "I'm just trying to do the right thing. For everyone."

He searched my face, and for a moment I thought he was going to catch onto my ploy. I wasn't the least bit sorry, but I had to let him think he had complete control. He had to think he won.

His eyes shifted and a shadow lifted behind them. He blinked and took a step back. "I'm sorry for giving you attitude."

I smiled a soft smile and let myself exhale a long breath. "Won't you let her come with us? Just for the night?"

He turned and looked at his daughter, dirt smudged on her cheeks. She should have been wearing a jacket, but she wasn't. "Madison," he said. "What do you want to do?"

She looked at him, then at my sister, and then at me, away from the porch and standing in the rain. I stared at her, hard, as if I could force my thoughts into her head. Finally, in the boldest, yet tiniest of voices, she said, "I want to sleep at Miswissa's house."

Without a word, William's eyes rolled toward the door, his chin followed, then he turned and stomped inside, letting the screen door slam behind him.

Mary Beth and I faced each other. She looked shocked and betrayed. I was confused until I realized she believed my apology was sincere, too. Like him, she was expecting me to match aggression with aggression. She had never seen a woman take on an abuser and win.

William returned with Madison's jacket in his hand and tossed it at my sister. "I want to talk to her before she goes to sleep," he said, jaw rigid, eyes avoiding mine.

My sister nodded in compliance as I scooped up Madison to strap her into the car seat before he could change his mind.

The sky darkened as we drove to my house, Mary Beth and Madison in the van, the broken television in the backseat of my car, a reminder to my sister in the weeks to come of the kind of man she had left behind.

I shivered in my wet clothes and turned up the heat. It wasn't over for her, just like my first-class flight out of El Paso didn't mean it had been over for me. But I felt a small sense of accomplishment knowing the two of them would be safe in my home, that I could provide them with shelter. Maybe it would give my sister the strength to stay away, just like moving home to my parents and not back to New Mexico had helped me.

I continued to shift my eyes to the rearview mirror, constantly checking for the minivan behind me. It wasn't until she pulled into the driveway that I was certain she wouldn't go back. The three of us, wet and tired, gathered in the kitchen together, peeled off our jackets, and stepped out of our soggy shoes.

"I've got to find some place to live," she said, rifling through a duffle bag for Madison's pajamas. She hadn't been to my house since Dave moved out, so she hadn't seen the work I had done to make it better.

"Come with me." I led her down the hallway to the guest room. I opened the door to the futon and dresser. "You can stay here as long as you need." My voice was strong and assured at her back as she stood in front of me and looked around. "It's not much, but Madison can share the bed with you until we figure something else out. There's room in the dresser and closet. We can store your extra stuff in the garage or the basement. I have a lot of extra room now."

My stick-like sister with her stringy wet hair walked into the freshly painted, newly carpeted room and sat on the edge of the bed. She lowered her chin, and I watched her face pinch into a deep and exaggerated frown, the way she had always done before she would begin to cry, even as a child. This was worse than a torn blanket or a lost doll.

"Mommy?" Madison pushed around my frame in the doorway and crawled onto the futon next to my sister. "Why are you sad?"

Mary Beth couldn't speak because once she did, the sobbing would come on with full force.

"Sometimes mommies get sad," I said quickly. "Your mommy has had a hard day."

Madison looked at me, then turned back to Mary Beth and tried to push her mother's head up so she could look at her crying face.

Mary Beth hugged her, and I watched the two of them cling to each other until she glanced up at me and said, "Thank you for the room."

By the end of spring, Mary Beth and I had settled into a steady routine of working nearly opposite schedules and occasionally meeting up at the kitchen table, seated across from each other on our respective laptops and cell phones, sharing stories, funny videos, and giggling or crying over the men who made infrequent and short-lived guest appearances in our lives.

She argued with William daily, sometimes all day, exchanging cruel and harassing text messages when they got too tired of fighting on the phone and hanging up on one another. My sister was making progress in her own way, though it was fitful and sporadic like she was learning to drive for the first time. Shaky, uncertain, fumbling, too cautious, naïve, and bumpy—she was all of those things, yet hopeful, too.

I wanted her to meet someone new, and sometimes she did, but her priorities were elsewhere. Living in my house made Mary Beth want her own, and without a man getting in the way; she started to consider there were more options than a one-bedroom apartment or a friend's basement.

Madison was growing and too headstrong and stubborn to share a bedroom with her mother among misshapen duffle bags stuffed with a mix of clothes for all seasons, the closet too small to hold them all. The nights were the worst for them when Madison didn't want to go to bed by herself and my sister couldn't watch yet another Disney movie and begged her toddler to stop jumping on the bed and just go to sleep.

Mary Beth started house hunting during the summer, and as fall drew near, she made an offer on a dated but sturdy three-bedroom ranch, a home they could grow into and find comfort in their own rooms and shared spaces.

The day Mary Beth began loading boxes into her van to take them to her new home, she received a call with a job offer for a new full-time position that paid a few thousand dollars more a year, putting her money concerns to rest.

She was doing it; she was surviving.

Part II
Tributaries

Chapter Seven

It was August. The midnight air cooled the sticky discomfort of the late summer day as we rode in the car with the windows down. In the passenger seat, I rested my head on the edge of the door; the wind sobering and soothing against my face.

Drunk. I wasn't, and then I was. Everything hummed around me in pieces. A moment in a bar. People I knew. Others who knew the people I knew, but I didn't know them. Introductions, forgotten names. The bill was paid without me noticing, my drinks and salad on someone else's credit card.

My reality was a patchwork quilt, a compilation of pieces, ripped and cut and sewn, coming together to make some sense of how I ended up in a car with three men ten years younger than me, just barely old enough to drink themselves. A love affair with alcohol had left gaps in my memory and the ability to reason, the stitching coming undone, the fabric unraveling.

"Hey guys," I said. My great idea compelled me to sit up and turn my head toward them. "So, I'm too drunk to drive home, right? I was thinking we should stop at a liquor store and get some beer. I'll buy."

The one driving laughed. "You're going to drink beer while you sober up?" He slapped his hand against the steering wheel and adjusted the volume on the radio.

"That's genius. Oh my god, Melissa, will you marry me?" In the backseat, one of them took off his seatbelt and knelt on the floor. "Look, I got down on one knee and everything. Please say yes."

I responded by accepting the proposal with a smile and question. "So does that mean we're stopping for beer?"

The marriage joke didn't end that night because within a few weeks, Joe—the backseat suitor— signed a lease to rent the guest room in my house. Almost immediately, the home took on an air of domesticity, as though we were actually in a loveless, sexless marriage with little communication, but maintaining a household together, nonetheless. We were two introverts who shared silence and respected each other's privacy so much that we often found ourselves on different floors of the house and going days, weeks, without talking in person.

It was September. An hour before the tenth anniversary of my twenty-first birthday party, a storm ripped through the city. Relentless rains and winds tore down tree limbs, shingles, and the utility pole in the backyard, leaving streets flooded for the night and houses without electricity for five days.

People showed up for the party anyway. "You have free beer," someone told me. "The party will go on."

And go on it did.

As the night dried up, more and more party-goers moved outside to escape the humidity building in the house. The downed power lines in the backyard pushed us into the driveway where we huddled in a circle on the concrete. A few of us took blankets to wrap around our shoulders, the combination of cool sidewalk beneath our jeans and iced beer bottles in our fists brought on shivers.

Scott was drunk, and when he was drunk, he got angry. His eyes scanned the collection of driveway dwellers and focused on Davey and Nick who were propped up against the bumper of Joe's car, snuggling under a blanket. Jealousy bubbled as he shouted at the two of them, unable to mask his long-time love for Davey, his ex-girlfriend turned best friend and roommate.

I stood up and let the blanket fall around me. Resting one hand in the palm of the other, I said, "Scott, you need to calm down."

"You don't understand! Davey only cares about Davey. Look at them. Right in front of my face! I should just go home."

He didn't back away even after I moved closer. I was within hitting distance but more worried his shouting would draw attention from the neighbors.

"You know you're in no condition to drive."

Scott's eyes were dark and glassy, and he leaned slightly forward, swaying gently like the bow of a tree, the alcohol searing through his veins.

"I've walked home from here before. Nobody cares, Davey doesn't care—" He looked down to where Davey sat, but she and Nick had since relocated to the couch in the basement, leaving me to deal with Scott on my own.

Our toes were practically touching. I was alone with this man known for violent outbursts when drunk, and defending the integrity of a mutual friend who had abandoned me for the safety of my home.

"Hey man." I sensed Joe just behind my right shoulder, literally backing me up, his voice low. "Relax. Come on. It's her birthday."

I closed my eyes and waited for one of them to throw a fist, knowing full well the only thing between them was me.

Instead, Joe continued to talk, his voice languid, the words leaving no room for dispute. Instead of getting punched, I found myself being hugged while Scott sobbed apologies against my ear. I turned and saw Joe next to me, my face full of unasked questions. He was the first man who had ever come to my rescue in an escalating situation without actually rescuing me.

When Joe was arrested two weeks later for driving while intoxicated, the police officer was not amused nor impressed with his ability to handle himself under the influence. It was raining the morning I drove him to the impound lot to get his car. My windshield wipers whined as they tried to keep visibility, an overcast sky adding glare and distraction. Joe rarely spoke under normal circumstances, but his silence morphed into a new shape. It took up its own space in the car between us like steam from a screaming kettle that neither could remove from the fire.

We got turned away twice before he could get his car. Once because he needed cash, the second time because the tank was empty. It drained while the car sat running on the side of the street, Joe passed out drunk in the driver's seat, facing west on an eastbound road. Joe didn't know this until he met with a lawyer and got a copy of the police report. He didn't remember driving the car at all, passing the exit to our home, and continuing on the freeway, getting further and further away while I slept, the night quiet outside my window.

Early on, one late and drunken night as the sun appeared on the horizon, I pointed an accusatory finger at Joe.

"You weren't there for me when I needed you."

He turned his head, and I thought I saw tears. I knelt on the floor next to him and apologized, over and over; I apologized because it was against everything in me to cause a grown man to cry especially one who had been so good to me while owing me nothing.

"Come here," he whispered, took my hand, and pulled me onto his lap. I draped my arms across his shoulders. He kissed me lightly on the cheeks and the forehead, then gently touched the tip of his nose to mine, his hand cupping the back of my neck.

"I'll take care of you," he said. "I promise."

I nodded and expected him to lean in to kiss me for real, to take total advantage of my vulnerability and need for comfort, but he didn't. Instead, he led me to my room, put me to bed, and stayed with me until I fell asleep, promising, "I'm here for you. I'm here for you."

Some months later someone asked me, "Do you think on some level he loves you?"

I didn't even have to pause. "I think he loves me on many levels. But not the one where he is in love with me."

However, I didn't relay the night he made his promise to me, a commitment even greater than the joking marriage proposal. No, I kept that night to myself, close to my heart.

*

November. There were grocery bags sitting on the floor of my kitchen that I filled with items belonging to a man I was trying to kick out of my life. A toothbrush, deodorant, pajama pants, a hand-made stuffed rabbit sewn together by an ex-girlfriend. Don't forget the blanket he brought over to wash and never took home, or the hoodie he always wore because I kept the thermostat low even with winter approaching.

I was too angry to feel sad. Instead, determination and fury kept me moving, taking care to keep CDs from scratching, book pages from tearing. I may have been angry, but I wasn't destructive.

Joe came home and noticed the emptiness left behind where a man once was. He sat at the dining table, playing music on his computer with the volume turned low. It was our sign, an invitation to talk. Waiting was his way of saying, "I'm here to listen if you need me." Joe's presence was a comfort but also a nagging reminder of what it meant to be accountable to someone else, how easy it was to lose myself if people weren't ever-present. He was to me what I needed from a man who wanted nothing from me.

I sat across from him, and put my head down, the tablecloth scratchy beneath my cheek.

"It's over." I would say it again. The scene would replay with other men who would leave, or I would leave them, or we would abandon each other. Some I would let go of quickly, easily, one would disappear completely, never to be heard from again, and another would leave me in a spinning state of drunken depression that lasted for days. But no matter how many times, no matter how many men, Joe would always appear at the table, the music down low, and wait until I was ready to talk.

"We should get a dog," Joe suggested after a friend of his adopted a husky puppy from a breeder in Detroit's Mexicantown. We were both so terribly unhappy that we wore our contempt for the world like a badge. A puppy, he suggested, was exactly the distraction we needed.

We? I asked myself. *We don't do anything together.* "That's the craziest thing I've ever heard," I said. "We are *not*, under any circumstances, getting a dog."

"We should get a dog," he repeated. We needed something to keep us going.

*

Three days later in Mexicantown, we stood in front of a tri-story house that looked as if no one was home; in fact, it looked as though no one had been home for years.

"Are you sure this is it?" I looked around and saw more of nothing except for an abandoned brick building across the street and debris collecting in overgrown flower beds that were dreary and withered with the onset of winter.

"This is the address they gave me." Joe shrugged in his unzipped black leather jacket with a baseball hat on his head, the brim pulled slightly to one side. It was warm, especially for the first of December. I wasn't even a little cold in a black-and-white cardigan sweater, having forgotten my wool coat draped over the back of my office chair in the rush to leave.

A white van pulled up next to the curb, and a young woman with dark hair climbed out. She smiled at us and nodded slightly as she passed through the gate and closed it behind her, disappearing into the backyard. I looked over at Joe as if to say, "What now?" but his face was already saying it.

Moments later, she returned with her arms wrapped around three squirming puppies, each just eight weeks old. She dropped them to the ground and latched the fence behind her.

From the backyard, we heard incessant barking and howling, the mother wondering where her little ones had gone. The puppies responded in kind with high-pitched whimpering as they clamored at the gate, digging and scratching, desperate to return to her.

We stood together and watched the puppies fumble over one another, two boys and a girl. Three days prior, getting a dog wasn't even a consideration. At that moment, leaving without one wasn't a possibility.

I bent over and scooped up the mongrel that had separated from the group. He was a mix of white and gray, with a solid black head, save for a white zigzag stripe between his eyes. The pup snuggled into me and stuck his wet nose in the crook of my neck.

Joe grinned.

"But I wanted a girl." It was barely a protest.

Joe raised his eyebrows and smiled wider.

I looked up at the woman. "A hundred dollars, right?"

She nodded and stuck her hand out. She may not have spoken English, but she definitely spoke money.

We laid a blanket down in the backseat, but the puppy disregarded it, preferring instead to run from one door to the other, pausing only long enough to put his paws up on the window, and twist his head back and forth while he watched a new world come to life through the glass.

"What are we going to name him?" Joe glanced in the rearview mirror. The dog bounced around the backseat, wrestling with the blanket.

A few half-hearted suggestions were tossed around, but none of them really stuck. I thought of the doberman named Princess I had while growing up, and Duchess, my dad's dachshund when he was a child. The husky in the back of Joe's car was the next in a long line of canine royalty.

"How about Duke?"

The pup jumped the distance to the front seat and scrambled to get his balance on the armrest between us before being nudged back.

"Duke," Joe tried it out. "I like Duke."

"I like Duke, too," I said, as his royal highness pounced on the seatbelt buckle then flopped down with a sigh.

When we arrived home, Joe and I knelt together, side by side in my bathroom, our sleeves pushed up, massaging puppy shampoo into Duke's thick fur as he struggled in the water, scrambling and fighting, his nails clicking against the bottom of the bathtub. The lather piled up and caught dirt that had settled in deep from spending the first two months of his life living in a dusty backyard.

"He needs his nails trimmed," Joe remarked. I pushed a soapy finger into the tip of my nose as if to say, "Not it!" and Duke took it as a cue to scramble out of the tub. We grabbed him together and wrestled him back down while I poured one cupful of water after another over his back. White fur emerged as dirty water splashed beneath him.

After Duke was fully rinsed, Joe lifted him out of the tub and we rubbed him dry with a towel while he crouched on the bathroom floor, panting.

Downstairs in the kitchen, I poured his over-sized bag of puppy food into a storage bin, the kibble forming a mound as the bag emptied. Duke stuck his nose into the bin, knocked some food to the floor and started munching, the bin just a little shorter than him.

"It's not a buffet," I said but didn't push him away.

After he had his fill, he wandered into the crate, circled twice, flopped down, and fell asleep.

"We have a dog," Joe said, as we stood together and watched our puppy sigh and snore.

March. Joe was on the cusp of a would-be relationship. Often I didn't even know she spent the night until the next morning when I saw her shoes by the front door. That was how I learned who she was: Tall black boots, yellow sandals, hand-painted canvas slip-ons. She had red flip-flops, too, until one morning when Duke chewed them into so many pieces that she had to walk home barefoot, hoping the whole time no one noticed that her not-boyfriend's dog scattered her shame all over his not-wife's kitchen floor.

Michelle's heart valves only opened for Joe. There were many nights where we found ourselves seated around the table, talking and drinking, laughing into darkness. Michelle and Joe shared a bed. Joe and I shared a home and a dog. Michelle and I shared a friendship. We were a Three's Company of contemporary America positioned in a Detroit suburb on the fringe of hope and wantonness. Despite our love for each other, we were all too frightened by what that meant to ever talk about it, no matter how much we drank.

She often confided in me about Joe, speculating as women do, as to why he wouldn't commit, why he wouldn't make it official. After all, everything between them pointed to a relationship. But I didn't raise the issue with him. I hid behind the veil of respecting his privacy, but the truth was more that I feared jeopardizing our relationship than I cared about preserving theirs. I couldn't sacrifice him for her happiness, and I couldn't watch her suffer because of his failure to commit to anyone but me.

In the meantime, our puppy was growing. I couldn't carry him like a stack of books with one arm anymore. He learned how to go upstairs, and finally got the courage to go down them as well. Duke could jump onto furniture without any assistance. At night, he shared my bed the most and developed his attachment to me more than Joe.

I taught him the practicalities of "sit" and "lie down," but Joe taught Duke to shake, fist bump, and catch a treat in the air. We sent each other picture messages of Duke doing cute things, obnoxious things, I-love-our-dog things, your-dog-is-in-trouble things. Our communication, our lives, were centered almost entirely on the dog. I wondered if Joe realized that someday he would move out, and when he did, Duke would remain with me, and I would be with the one with a dog's life of companionship. Joe would carry on. Alone.

May. I attempted a new relationship that required me to disappear on the weekends, chasing love for hours on a freeway toward a man who lived in another state. While traveling south to cross the state of Ohio, I thought of Raul each time I passed the exit to the old studio apartment. I remembered clawing at a Ph.D. pipe dream and curling into a ball on my bath mat, sobbing because of Raul's control over me from thousands of miles away.

In contrast, the scenery along the freeway was always beautiful, lush and green with tall swaying trees that invited any traveler to take their exits and explore the little college town rich in both history and angst.

I gnawed on my bottom lip until I got to the edge of Cincinnati and crossed the bridge into northern Kentucky, the water calm and serene, the river doubling as the state line. During my weekend visits, we attended festivals along the bank, sat by the water's edge and watched the Cincinnati crown change colors from a distance. Joe stayed behind with the dog, and only ever asked me one question: "When are you coming home?"

On the riverbank, we interlaced our fingers and thought I had finally found a good man. My friends told me so, as many of them were friends with him, too. Together, we walked the path at the Cincinnati Zoo and stood in line for twenty minutes to feed a cracker to a giraffe. We both grinned at the new zoo babies and remarked how all animals are sweet and lovable when they are young. He suggested I bring Duke on the next visit, and we discussed the different things we could do on a weekend with a dog in tow. I thought of the three of us walking the bike path along the Cincinnati River and mused *that's what happiness, what family, must feel like.*

Then that same man shut down the relationship before things started to go wrong, providing explanations that didn't make sense, reasons I couldn't process. I argued with him, actually argued, to get him to reconsider, to realize we had something good and real together. That's what I wanted, so why didn't he want the same thing? He didn't budge on his position. His declaration wasn't "we should break up," but instead, "I want to break up," as if I didn't have a say in the matter, and the truth was just that; I didn't. When one person decides to end the relationship, the other person doesn't get to rebut the decision; instead, she just finds herself single against her will.

I returned home, rested my head on the kitchen table, and looked to Joe to explain what went wrong this time. He didn't have an answer.

"You deserve better," he said. "You deserve better."

But what does better look like?

That weekend, I took Duke to the lake by my parents' house and tossed a tennis ball into the water. The dog who hated to be bathed lunged after it, paddling through the murk, scooped the ball up in his jaw and brought it back to me. We played the game all afternoon while my brothers and nephews splashed in the lake together and my parents watched from a park bench. At sunset, my sister-in-law took a picture of Duke and me on the beach. The dog had replaced the man in pictures and my life.

August. I was pulled from sleep on a Thursday night by Michelle and our friend Austin standing next to my bed.

"Wake up! Time to go out!" Austin said, laughing his Austin laugh and smiling the way he does when he is making a sales pitch.

"It's Tony's birthday," Michelle continued, taking the approach that if they provided me with an explanation, a reasonable explanation, then I would concede. Tony was a friend of theirs, though. I had only met him a few times.

I shooed them away and rolled over, my protests muffled by the messy piles of sheets and blankets lumped all over my bed. From the kitchen I heard the others—Tony, Jamiil, and Brian—shout my name over and over until I sat up and agreed to go, but just for a little while, an hour at most.

We started at a small bar in town with a beer, and within an hour found ourselves handing our keys to the valet outside a gay bar in Detroit where Michelle, Austin, and I waited in line for drinks hand-poured by a drag queen. The rest of our group wandered off to dance on a platform next to the DJ booth or outside to take selfies next to a fountain.

We stayed until just minutes before the bar closed, the last few people on the dance floor, the hours spent there ignored and not discussed as time to wake up for work drew closer. On the way home, the six of us crammed into the extended cab of Brian's pickup truck. Tony barely made it inside my home before he lifted the lid of the trashcan and threw up every fruity birthday shot we bought him throughout the night.

I felt instantly sober, barking directions at my friends to get a washcloth, a towel, a glass of water. Duke whined in his crate and someone let him outside. I threw Tony's clothes in the washing machine to rid them of sweat and vomit.

Joe came out of his room and a chorus of apologies rose up from the group for waking him. As the night wore on, Tony was barely conscious and everyone else had scattered to couches or mattresses throughout the house. Michelle brought a sleeping bag and a spare pillow from a closet, Austin wrapped the pillow with a towel, and we put Tony to bed on the kitchen floor. He started to vomit but didn't wake up.

"He's going to choke in his sleep," I said and asked for a blanket and a pillow, then I was on the floor next to Tony, nodding off slowly, getting pulled out of sleep every few minutes to prop him up and hold a bucket under his chin.

Everyone had gone to sleep except Joe who was standing in the kitchen, leaning against the counter, and not saying a word.

"Where's Michelle?" I asked him.

"She's sleeping in your room."

I settled back down on the floor, grateful I had mopped it that afternoon.

"What is your problem, anyway?" I asked him. "Why don't you just go for it with her?"

He didn't say anything.

"This isn't one of those times where you can get away with not answering."

His voice was a whisper, "I'm afraid of screwing it up."

I closed my eyes and rested my head on the pillow. When I opened them again, Joe was still standing there, looking at the floor in front of him, but not at me. Not at me.

"You need to fix this, Joe," I told him with my eyes closed. I was slurring my words, but I wasn't slurring the truth. He knew it, too. "She loves you. *Loves* you. And you treat her like crap."

From him I got silence, vacant nodding, and a clenched jaw.

"I don't interfere in your life very often. So when I do, it should count for something."

Thirty minutes later, I woke up to hold the bucket for Tony, and Joe was still standing there to make sure we were both okay. His loyalty to me mirrored Duke's. But just to me. Not to Michelle.

Chapter Eight

I lifted the pistol in front of me and held it at arm's length with elbows locked, trying to remember all the instructions Glen had given me. *Look here. Aim there. Release the slide. Hold with your hand like this. Cup with your other hand here. Then place your finger on the trigger and squeeze toward you, slowly, slowly,* click, *slowly,* fire.

A burst of dust exploded from a mound of dirt inside The Pit, an outdoor public shooting range that looked like the steep side of a ravine. The recoil was so hard that it forced me to close my eyes. I fired again, and again closed my eyes. Again. Still again. I shot a whole magazine in the direction of targets and empty boxes, old trash cans, and tattered litter scattered about the range. Each time I squeezed, I fired into darkness. It was like trying to keep my eyes open while I sneezed. Physically impossible.

Glen's warnings and coaching echoed in my head with each shot. *A gun won't shoot itself. Guns don't just "go off" like in the movies. You have to release the slide and then pull the trigger. But make sure the safety is on anyway when you're not using it. Always point the barrel away from people, even when you think you're out of ammo, even when the gun isn't loaded.*

I felt adrenaline build in my chest and surge throughout my body. This was a *gun* with *bullets.* A handgun that was only used for one thing: to shoot other people. Everything else was just target practice.

Removing my finger from the trigger, I lowered the gun, released the magazine, and began to reload it. I picked up the individual rounds and let them roll around in my palm, the metal cool and smooth against my skin. Individually, they didn't feel threatening, not like something that had the potential to pierce flesh, rip through organs, and take life. Why did I fear the gun and not the ammo? Which was more dangerous? More threatening? In my mind you couldn't shoot a gun without ammo, but you couldn't shoot ammo without a gun. They were a set, like lock and key.

"What do you think?" Glen asked as he set up and organized a row of rifles along the stone wall that separated the shooters from the targets.

I looked down at the gun in my hand. There was grime under my fingernails, and I could feel the dirt in my teeth. The air around us was cool and breezy as summer inched toward fall. The Pit rose up in front of us at least five stories, full of small hills and valleys, tree roots and bushes. It was a natural wonderland, and we were shooting at it.

"This gun is too, I don't know," I said, feeling its pressing weight in my hand. "It's too big. I can't shoot it without closing my eyes."

Glen gave me a doubtful look. "What do you mean you're closing your eyes? How do you see where you're shooting?"

"I guess I don't." I raised the gun and fired again, and again, closed my eyes.

*

"When are we going shooting?" It was a question I was used to hearing. Whenever we spent more than an hour together, Glen would raise the issue.

"I have no interest in shooting a gun."

The exchange was scripted by then.

"*Why not?*"

I would sigh, shrug my shoulders, and give the same answer. "I don't like guns."

Though that wasn't necessarily true. It wasn't that I didn't *like* guns. It was more that I was afraid of them. My fear had evolved into a very anti-gun standpoint. The adage "guns don't kill people, people kill people," was revised in my mind as "people with guns kill people; therefore, people shouldn't have guns."

Glen—a heavily tattooed punk-looking thirty-year-old— who took my Composition class at the community college compelled me to reconsider my position on guns and gun ownership. When I met him, he was married, his wife pregnant. By the time the semester ended, the baby had been born, but Glen and his wife were separated. When the winter snow melted and the onset of spring meant outdoor shooting season, Glen was no longer married. He dated casually at first, but was regretting the divorce within six months.

At first his reasoning was because of his son.

"At the very least, we need to learn to parent together. We can't even talk to each other without it turning into an argument. That's not good for Dayde."

Then it was for Jessie.

"Yes, we were only married a year, but we had been together ten years before we got married. Obviously, she is a big part of my life. I just need to get her to trust me again. Maybe I wasn't there for her when Dayde was born in the way that she needed me to be. Maybe she has a point."

Then it was for himself.

"I want to feel confident that I did everything I could do to make it work."

We were around the same age and the teacher-student dynamic ended when final grades were submitted. Glen and I would meet up for dinner and drinks sporadically—sometimes weekly, sometimes months would pass before we would reconnect. Although our relationship was platonic, the conversations were often inundated with innuendo. Glen had a knack for spinning our conversation toward sex, and no aspect of that topic was off-limits. We had a dynamic that didn't make sense to anyone else, and for us, it worked that way.

As the months accumulated and our friendship strengthened, Glen relentlessly pursued Jessie, and I continued to cycle through failed attempts at finding a good man. Each time another one of my relationships would end, he was there offering advice and friendship.

After I had a particularly difficult breakup, he drove the twenty miles from his house on a Tuesday to drag me out to our favorite bar, plunk me down at a table on the outdoor patio, and put forth every attempt to make me smile. When that didn't work, he bought me drinks and told stories I had heard dozens of times until they were funny again, and I couldn't help but cheer up.

Likewise, whenever Jessie gave him even a hint of hope that their marriage had a second chance but then took it away, I would sit across a table from him and listen. He had a gregarious personality that pulled me in, and I had the ability to be empathetic and compassionate without pitying him. His friends were less patient with his relationship situation, and many of them urged him to move on.

"Have you ever thought of dating Mel?" one of them asked him two years after we had become close friends. They all knew me as Mel, which is the only way Glen had ever addressed me, even in the classroom.

"Mel? I would feel less weird about sleeping with my step-sister."

When Glen told me the story, I had a good laugh right along with him knowing I didn't see him as dating potential either, and I had said so to my friends who had also suggested it.

We had trusted each other with revelations about our choices and failures, some details so personal that we had never revealed the truth to anyone else. Yet, the only thing we seemed to have in common was failed relationships and our polarized opinions about guns.

"Let me take you shooting," he urged. "I'll show you everything you need to know. Guns are safe if you know how to use them."

I shook my head. "I don't need to shoot a gun."

Though, his arguments were starting to sink in. If there was anyone I could trust to put a gun in my hand, it was Glen. We both knew that.

*

It was obvious I didn't know what I was doing. Feeling tired and uncomfortable, I just wanted to sit and watch, but there was nowhere to sit and really nothing to watch. I finished shooting the round in Glen's handgun, released the magazine, and placed the two pieces away from each other on the ledge in front of me.

"You done?" Glen was counting bullets before loading the ammo into a magazine.

"Yeah," I finally said, the answer covered in layers of hesitation and doubt.

"What's wrong?"

"It's too much. I don't like how it makes me feel. Even after shooting it for a while, I'm still scared of it. And isn't that the whole point? So I won't be scared anymore?"

"Want to try this one?" Glen asked before he knelt down and peered through the scope of an AR-15, a semi-automatic assault rifle.

I shrugged. "Sure."

He walked me through the process again, how to load, how to aim, how and when to squeeze the trigger. I closed my left eye, took aim, and *ping*, I shot into the ground. Leaning back a little, I looked at Glen. "That's it?"

He laughed. "The ammo for this one is much smaller."

I shook my head. "So, it isn't the size of the gun that matters? It's the size of the bullets?"

"Sometimes it's not about size at all." He winked.

Glen picked up the handgun and started to load it. While I struggled to force each round into the magazine, he filled it effortlessly, metal sliding against metal and clicking into place. Glen dropped the gun into its holster and positioned himself in front of The Pit. He did a few shoulder rolls and let his hands hang at his side then closed his eyes and stood there, his body still and waiting.

I wasn't sure what he was doing or about to do, but didn't say anything to him.

Another shot was fired into The Pit and Glen reacted. He grabbed the gun from the holster, and moved along the wall, taking aim and firing one round after the other, bullets ripping through boxes, plastic bottles, mounds of dirt, and dented beer cans. He stopped when he was out of rounds, and a haze of dust rose above the assaulted targets.

"I hit almost all of them," he said with a laugh, releasing the magazine to load it again.

I wondered how much he had to practice to become so skilled, so efficient, and so confident. There wasn't anything in my life that I was that good at. Slightly shaking my head, the self-doubt lowered my shoulders. I would probably never be able to get to a point where I could stand still, take aim, and withstand the recoil and hit a target, let alone hit one while moving.

"Want to try again?"

I looked at the gun as he held it out to me. "The recoil—"

"Try it again," he said. "I'll show you some things that might work this time."

I nodded and reached for the gun. The student had become the teacher.

*

Upon moving into an apartment after my divorce, I had a house-warming party in which, at some point that night, I was seated on the couch and holding a gun for the first time. I was twenty-five, living in downtown Las Cruces, and was dizzy drunk.

All the party guests had gone home except for one. Raul returned from his car with a black case tucked under one arm and a sleeping bag in the other. We were barely friends at this point, and in fact, that night, he was pining for Jodi and hoping to go home with her. Instead, she convinced him to stay, to look after me and make sure I was of sound enough mind to go to sleep and still wake up in the morning.

"What is that?"

He looked to where I was pointing. "My gun. I don't want to leave it in the car."

My eyes widened. "You can't bring a gun in here." I punctuated each word.

He sat down next to me and opened the case, causing me to cringe and back away from him.

"It's not loaded," he chuckled and held it out to me.

I looked at him and then down at the gun.

"Here," he said. "Just hold it."

I moved my hand toward him but didn't quite open it, didn't quite invite the gun in.

"Go ahead. Shoot it."

Sweat gathered at the nape of my neck, and I looked away from him. "I don't want to."

"Just try it. Nothing will happen. You'll see." He took my hand and pulled it upward and forward, the gun aimed at a mirror on the other side of the room. He tapped my finger to inch it closer to the trigger.

I felt the curve of the metal against the inside of my hand. A twitch, and a *click*. Nothing.

"I told you," he mocked.

That night I slept a restless sleep, the weight and feel of the gun still a memory in my hand when I woke up in the morning.

*

"If I can get the skeet launcher to work, you should try that," Glen said, examining a shotgun.

"Skeet?" I asked. Was that another one of his sexual references?

"Yeah, you know. Pigeons. Clays?" He pointed to a cardboard box resting on the ledge with pictures of discs printed on the side of it. "You want to try it?"

I nodded. The other guns were still lined up on the ledge, and there were plenty of cases of ammo ready to be loaded. It would be a while before Glen was ready to leave.

He tested the launcher's release mechanism. Once satisfied that it was working, Glen loaded six clays and propped the shotgun up against my shoulder. "Pump and shoot," he said, then laughed at the implicit double-meaning of the statement.

"That's it?"

He shrugged. "Pretty much. Try it once, and if you like it, I'll show you how to reload."

The spring released, and the pigeon flew in front of me in various directions. I squeezed the trigger, and the recoil jerked my shoulder back. Grunting, I clenched the gun tighter as the booming sound of the fired shotgun echoed throughout The Pit. *That* was power.

"Again," I said, and positioned the gun against my shoulder, ready to aim and fire at another.

The discs spun into the air, and I pumped the gun and fired, three— sometimes four—times before they hit the ground and broke into tiny pieces. Each time I gripped the barrel and pumped it back, power surged throughout my arms, my muscles tensed and flexed, my anticipation heightened for the next launch. I went through a box of a hundred clays before I was ready to quit. Even though I didn't hit a single one of them, my confidence grew with each new round in the chamber.

After another hour, we packed up the guns and ammo, and drove away from The Pit. I offered to pay Glen for the ammo and pigeons, but he dismissed my offer with a wave of his hand.

"I'm glad you finally did it," he said. "I know you were nervous and unsure of what to expect."

"I'm glad I did, too." I studied my grimy hands. "It was definitely an experience."

Glen pulled up to a stop sign and checked both ways for oncoming traffic. "You're not convinced?"

I pressed my fingertips to the half-dollar-sized bruise forming just below my collarbone from the shotgun. "It just isn't for me. I learned a lot and don't feel afraid the way that I did before. I just don't have much interest in going again. I don't think."

Glen leaned back in the driver's seat and angled toward me a little. "I can respect that," he said. "It's not for everyone."

"I did like the shotgun, though," I said with a definitive nod. "It was fun shooting those clays."

Glen chuckled. "Of all the guns you shot today, I had no idea that one would be your favorite."

"It gave me a hickey." I touched the spot below my collarbone again. "That's the most action I've had in months."

His chuckle turned into a laugh. "Glad I could help."

Chapter Nine

At 4:30 a.m., there was too much vodka but not enough beer. A disarray of playing cards that had been thrown down after each turn covered the coffee table. It was some kind of drinking game I didn't understand. Before the next round started, I walked toward the kitchen to refill my cup, squeezing around a beer pong table still set up from last night's party.

With my bare hand, I reached into the bag of ice split open in the kitchen sink, grabbed a fistful, dropped it into the glass, added vodka, and topped it off with tonic. I wished for a lime, though there didn't seem to be a place to cut it. The kitchen was filthy; garbage piled up in the corner because the guys ran out of trash bags and each swore it was the other one's turn to buy more. Most people I knew would clean up before a party, but this wasn't exactly a party. It was two roommates who each had a girl over for the night. I was one of the girls. This was River City.

Drake sat next to me on the couch, his body tall and lanky, wearing a T-shirt, baggy jeans, no socks. When he laughed, he pulled his knees up to his chest and curled forward. His hair swooped down and rested on heavy eyebrows, the ends gently curled upward that he would repeatedly brush aside. He clutched a whiskey and Coke, drinking down two to my one. Drake must not have understood the card game either because he lost a round, yelled "Fuck!" and took a drink.

"If anyone asks," he told me earlier, "you're twenty-six. No, twenty-seven. Yeah, you can pass for twenty-seven."

I was approaching my thirty-second birthday. My age, though, was a secret because there were too many years between us for him to be honest with himself and others about it. Who would ask? I wondered but didn't say it. Instead, I rolled my eyes and dismissed his request with my smile and a nudge to his shoulder.

*

Our first meeting had been a scheduled interview, a get-to-know-you that Drake had to complete for an assignment. I was used to those sessions by then, as he was the fourth young man who had sat across from me at my desk, and posed the standard questions, "What does your job entail?" and "How long have you lived in Michigan?" and "What do you think makes a mentor?" They were questions of polite distance, questions to pass the time.

His questions, however, skipped the preliminaries and got right to the heart of the matter. He asked the one question that always determined if he would open himself to others or not. "What kind of music do you listen to?"

I fumbled through an explanation, an apology almost, while describing a varied mix of eighties rock, forgotten ballads of the seventies, shamelessly catchy pop songs. "The music of underdogs," I finally said.

His expression changed. He sat back in his seat and the hood on his sweatshirt bunched around his shoulders.

"No way," he said, and at first, I thought he was making fun of my eclectic taste. But he wasn't. The laughter-like cadence of his voice rolled over me as we quoted song lyrics back and forth. Phil Collins. Depeche Mode. Meat Loaf. Duran Duran. He knew their music better than I did, as if he wasn't born fifteen years too late to appreciate.

"Music is iconic; it defines a generation," he said. "That's what every musician hopes happens to their music. That's really what they want."

Music was his religion. Music was his redemption. Music was how he survived.

*

He had potential and showed promise. But after our meeting, he disappeared for the summer and never returned. In the fall, I caught glimpses of baby blue hooded sweatshirts or black and green skate hats around campus, and for a moment, I thought it could be him. But it wasn't. I knew better. He had gone off to a more affordable state school some place that was too far away to matter.

Instead, Drake lived in my computer. He was nothing more than words exchanged on a screen, messages sent late into the night referencing a musician or inquiring about a limited release album, or a description of a tattoo he wanted to get, and would I take a road trip across the country with him to have it done?

Sometimes, our conversations were real time, pecked away while standing at a computer kiosk while my students diligently plugged away at their essays. Our conversations were lengthy, time-consuming, and frequent until they weren't. Then it could be weeks, months, or longer, of silence.

He needed to retreat. Occasionally it was drugs, sometimes booze, often music. When he really needed to hide, though, he escaped by long-boarding. I could imagine him moving along a Lake Michigan seawall, his strong, lean legs pushing him forward, an open shirt billowing around the soft, dark hair on his chest, an emerging manhood masking a post-teenage body. He would wear that same hat slightly pulled to one side, his hair bushed over his forehead, beaded sweat catching sunlight. His shouts and laughter would be lost in the wind as the waves lapped up onto the beach.

I pictured him hurdling off walkways, onto benches, and off again onto the concrete, sometimes landing the jump, sometimes not, his feet dancing across the board for show and balance. He would steady himself against the backdrop of the water, put his foot to the ground and press himself forward, leaning into the curve of the board, like a river cutting through the city.

*

Even though it was December, it was warm enough for me to sit on a deck for most of some party, drunk and propped up against a bannister, slightly aware that I didn't belong there. Drake was there. He wasn't supposed to be, though, because he didn't belong there anymore, either. There were no rivers in that city.

He appeared outside next to me. I threw my arms around him and pleaded with someone to take our picture.

"It's not weird, is it?" I didn't mean the photo. I meant seeing each other after the content of our most recent conversation. It was a flirtation that had turned hot and fiery and dangerous and wrong and ended almost as quickly as it had started.

He had panicked. Reneged.

"It was a fantasy," he said, "just a fantasy, and I used you. I almost used you. I almost used you for a dream. Besides, there's another girl, a girl I want to try and make it with, and I want to be fair to her. And to you. I just want to be fair."

At the party, he said, "No, it's not weird. It's fine." He hugged me tighter and smiled at the camera. The picture, like the evening, was a blur.

The last time I heard his voice that night was while he rubbed my back as I puked into a trash can.

"You're all right," he told me. Then a few minutes later, "I have to leave. They're calling me. I have to leave."

I raised my head long enough to see his red-sweater silhouette walking toward the front door. My eyes closed instead of watching him leave.

The next morning I woke up on the couch shivering under a thin blanket, my mouth dry and throat acidic. I could still smell him on my clothes. Stretching the fabric over my face, I inhaled, knowing it would soon fade.

*

For a year, I missed him. For half a year, I didn't even know his life. When his voice finally found my ear on the telephone, it was a recording. I was on a layover in the Pittsburgh airport, returning from a ten-day tour of Spain.

"I'm sorry. Please forgive me. I don't deserve it, I know. But I need to know you don't hate me. Please don't hate me. You must hate me. Even if you do, will you call me anyway?"

I sighed and deleted the message, knowing I would call him back later. He didn't have to beg. I always forgave him even before he made a mistake that fed the sadness. Even if I expressed anger, expressed disappointment, I didn't mean it. He would always come back, and when he did, I would be ready, waiting, accepting. Drake was a fixture of nostalgia, an insignia of what I could do well, of what I could do right. And that was to save people from themselves.

"Do you know what a man's biggest fear is?" Through the phone his voice was deep and genial with a hint of laughter, even in the seriousness of the question.

Rare early autumn sunlight filled the room around me as I sat in a chair next to a window; my body turned sideways with legs dangling over the arm. My Spain tan had finally faded, but the memory of the desperation in his voice had not. It was our first time communicating after weeks of being off-again. The unexpected silence was finally broken when he responded to text messages in which I practically berated him for not talking to me after he had been the one to reach out in the first place.

A lot of shit kinda transpired. I mean, a lot a lot.
What kind of shit?
Fuck-up-your-life shit is fucking-up-my-life shit.
Tell me.
I'm too ashamed to tell you.
You can tell me anything. I've never judged you, and I never will.
No response.

I sent him a question mark, nothing more.

The phone rang.

I skipped over greetings. "What's going on?"

He was quiet for a second, and when he finally spoke, his voice was low, though still distinctively his, and that was when he posed the question.

"Do you know what a man's biggest fear is?"

I was unable to answer at first, still caught up in the sound of his voice. It moved me in a way that no one else's could. I shifted in the chair until both my feet rested on the floor.

"I don't know," I said. "Death?"

"Getting a girl pregnant."

The words cut through every part of me, challenging the soft sunlight, my relaxed posture, my encouraging smile. I was not prepared for that level of revelation and definitely not ready to coax him through it.

"Oh, no," I said. "You didn't. When? Who?" The details didn't really matter but asking for them gave me time to process.

It was some neighbor girl, he explained, a girl who had offered herself to him and coaxed him to remove the condom. "I want to feel you," she had said.

Well, she felt him all right. All the way to the pharmacy to buy a test and all the way to the doctor's office to confirm the results.

They had slept together two weeks prior.

I told him that didn't add up. There was no way she would know so soon after. So either she was lying, or he was.

"Then why would she say that?"

"I don't know." Even when I was in my twenties, I had a hard time understanding the mindset of twenty-something women. "Maybe she's trying to get your attention."

"There are so many other ways to get my attention!" The words blended together in a panicked groan.

Symbols gave him comfort. There was nothing symbolic with her.

*

He opened the door to me standing on the porch and declared, "Now there's trouble in River City."

That was our joke. It didn't come from any significant place, but it was ours. We spoke in lyrics, in rhyme. Our dialogue was plagiarized, bastardized, glorified. Warmth penetrated our skin as our bodies pressed together, and the city would come alive with mischief and illusion.

The morning after the card game party, the ice was completely melted in the kitchen sink, and I was crouched in the corner of his room, stuffing dirty clothes and a half-empty vodka bottle into a duffle bag as quietly as possible, trying not to wake him as I prepared for my four-hour drive home.

"Can you stay a few more hours?" His voice was slightly muffled by the dozens of pillows and layers of blankets piled up around him.

"Sure," I said, and he quickly fell back asleep.

I stayed in bed next to him and watched the room expand and compress with his breath.

The morning spilled into the afternoon, and I finally coaxed him out of bed with an offer to buy lunch before leaving town. At the restaurant, we both wore hoodies, Greek letters stitched across our chests, elbows rested on the tabletop, the remains of lunch cooling in paper serving boats between us.

The ice settled in my glass as I sipped down the rest of my water. Our voices carried energy, magnetism between our bodies that could only be defined as unconditional trust.

He did most of the talking. I was strangely comforted by the delusion that I could pose as a college student in a college town, a sorority girl on a lunch date with her fraternity guy, miles away from anyone who would know any better or care.

With him, I didn't think about how our time was a façade, something that could never exist beyond the world we had created for one another.

I only focused on the wonderment of us, the unlikelihood we would ever be together in the way that we had been together, and our way didn't need definition or rationalization. It didn't have to make sense to anyone else or even to us.

I had moments where I envisioned a future, tried to picture times spent celebrating holidays with each other's families and even establishing a home. Those visions were hazy at best and short-lived. I had to cling to every moment spent with him, every time he confided in me about his dreams and fears. At that moment in the restaurant, it was just him and me, and that moment could last minutes or hours, but the time belonged to us.

The relationship may have seemed one-sided in Drake's favor, and maybe it was. Something about being with him, though, empowered me to endure challenges and feel deserving of something more than I had ever allowed for myself.

When I dropped him off at his apartment, I watched him walk inside and waited to see if he would turn and wave before the door closed behind him. He did, and when I returned the gesture, he gave me a smile and a nod of his chin before disappearing inside.

Everything became quiet while the sun set behind tall university buildings, the river splitting from its city. Driving away, I knew Drake would have to be the last man that I could love unconditionally. I had made progress by learning to love at all, and loving Drake was easy because he needed me, and I wanted to be needed. But it was time to make reparations with myself, to seek love that could be, would be, returned and not taboo.

Chapter Ten

He lives in a psychiatric ward. At least, that's what I thought the first time I walked into Ryan's apartment. It was our third date after meeting online, and he had invited me over for post-dinner drinks.

The rooms were contained within dingy white walls, and there were no more than six pieces of furniture in the entire place. Books seemed to be the only accessories, and I made note of the stacks in the corners, piles on the dining table, and rows bowing the shelves of a cheap wooden bookcase.

He had lived there for three years, but I wouldn't have known that unless he had told me. Ryan didn't want to get too locked into any place, and the best way to avoid that was to accumulate as little as possible. Most of the books, he said, had been checked out from the library. When they came due, they would leave emptiness in their place.

I bent over to untie my shoes and noticed an odd smell, a more pungent version of what came off his clothes when he hugged me. Inhaling, I got a nose full of the aftermath of candles when their aroma fades and the stale stench of old cigarette smoke emerges. He had been a non-smoker for two months, but his apartment was highly nostalgic and clung to the fading carcinogens. Had we met two months prior, there would have never been another date after the first ashtray-tasting kiss.

He gestured to the worn leather couch, and I sat down, sinking until my knees were chest-level. Ryan sat down next to me and turned on the television, a reflex that made me roll my eyes. When the TV is there, you must obey, I thought, and realized then why so many of the borrowed books sat in piles, unread.

I looked over at him, and he grinned at me with his lips pressed together. When he leaned in to kiss me, I tried not to fixate on how awkward the whole experience was, how forced it felt. After all, he was a nice guy. Why not give him a break?

It had taken a lot of convincing for me to try online dating sites. I expected them to be slightly more complex versions of the superficial chat rooms that peaked in popularity in the nineties among pedophiles, predators, sex addicts, and young and unattractive hopefuls. But I hadn't dated anyone seriously since Dave, and I was tired of casual encounters with long-time male friends that—despite my hopes and expectations—

never evolved into a commitment.

One of my friends recommended a site that worked for him, so I set up a profile that quickly filled my inbox with requests for naked photos and inquisitions into my sexual interests.

"Are you into bi-guys?" one had asked.

"I'm in an open relationship and looking for a secondary," another's blind optimism said.

There were plenty of unimaginative invitations for threesomes, too, because, "My wife really likes redheads."

Just like that, I had been ushered onto the battlefield of the casual sex revolution without realizing I had even enlisted. Most certainly, I didn't want another Raul, Dan, or even another Dave. I couldn't love without return the way I had done for Drake. There needed to be someone, something, different, but I had yet to be able to define that for myself.

By the time Ryan's greeting appeared in my inbox, I was jaded by the playful invitations and didn't expect to take him seriously.

In his slightly blurry profile picture, he was sitting with his back to an aluminum shelf full of textbooks, wearing a sweater. He looked like the kind of guy who played video games for hours and thought showers were optional, especially on the weekends.

Maybe he was the kind of thirty-something who still dressed like he had in high school, the awkward wardrobe choices that were almost two decades behind the rest of us. Something was off with his smile, too, though I couldn't quite tell if it was the picture or if there was something wrong with his face. I felt guilty for zeroing in on a possible imperfection but still hesitated before reading his message, which turned out to be long and conversational and expressed interest in me. Now this, I thought, was different.

I gave it a day before replying to him, and I only did so because he asked me questions that made specific reference to my profile, and I thought it would be unkind of me for him to do all that work only to have it ignored.

We exchanged emails for about a week before he invited me to coffee on a Saturday afternoon. I accepted his invitation, mostly because I enjoyed the stories in his lengthy and detailed messages. He offered to meet up in my neighborhood, and I agreed because it was the middle of January, and I didn't have any interest in driving twenty miles in the snow to his side of town, especially not for a coffee date. A full meal?

Maybe. But just coffee? Not a chance.

After ordering a chai latte, I slid into a booth near a window, watched the snow fall, and waited. I wasn't nervous, but instead worried I was wasting my time. The messages we'd sent back and forth replayed in my mind, and it occurred to me while sitting in the booth that I had agreed to meet him before ever talking to him on the phone. That realization only added to my doubt, and I thought about leaving. But he was driving there in a snowstorm, so it would be cruel to stand him up. I decided to give it an hour. If, after one hour, there was no connection, I would tell him so and walk out into the snow, back to my car, and return to the familiar comforts of my home.

I turned from the window to find a man standing at the table staring down at me, slightly fidgety, his expression unreadable. Startled at first, when I realized it was Ryan, I offered him a smile and an invitation to sit down. It wasn't until after he got his coffee—without offering me a second one—that I had the chance to study his face and saw the scars.

From the front, I saw skin between his nose and upper lip pulled tight, while the rest puffed out, reminding me of the snout on a pug puppy. When he turned to the side, his profile morphed into a more severe deformity. His nose was flat, the rounded fleshy tip almost entirely absent, his upper lip pulled straight. His lower lip—which was too big for his face—jutted out, making it appear as though he had an under-bite. When he gave any of my questions deep thought or consideration, he had a tendency to thrust his eyebrows downward and push his lip out further. He had a small smile—the scars around his lips making it impossible for them to stretch when he was happy or amused. Instead, he would press his lips together, laugh from his throat, and nod while his eyebrows bounced up and down.

He's ugly, I concluded, feeling disappointed and duped. Nice eyes, yes, and he was tall with broad shoulders, but I didn't find him attractive.

Instead of putting me off, though, he put me at ease. At least he had confidence, and I wanted to be the kind of person who didn't fixate on physical imperfections, because I knew from dating Raul how hurtful that was. So I sat across the table from him and talked for a few hours, finding myself sharing common professional ambitions and political affiliations. When it was time to leave, I initiated the hug good-bye. "We should meet up again sometime," I said.

"I like him," I told my sister one night when she called. We had gone out a few times by then to a restaurant, an ice sculpture festival, bowling. But what I was really saying, though, was that I *wanted* to like him.

"He's easy to talk to, and we laugh a lot. He's also an academic, so he understands my world, my passion for teaching."

I described the conversations we'd had, the way he seemed more interested in me as a person than most others. Then I told her about his scars and his defected speech, the way he had trouble pronouncing certain words that required him to push his tongue off the roof of his mouth, a limitation that was gradually wearing on me, no matter how much I tried to ignore it.

"So I'm worried," I told her.

"About what?"

Then I admitted to her what I was, until that moment, afraid to admit to myself. "I'm worried what people will think." I felt shallow saying it, but once it was out there, I couldn't take it back. "I wonder how my friends will react to him, how Mom and Dad will react to him. I'm worried they'll wonder what I see in him or something."

She was quiet for a moment, then said, "If he makes you happy, who cares what people think?"

"I know that in my head but you know it's not that easy."

"Well, if this guy is a '10' to you, the people in your life who care about you are going to see that. And they'll see him as a '10' as well."

This level of insight from her was unexpected, for she was someone whose own history with men was even more capricious than mine. I was stunned to silence.

We compared notes about our exes and agreed that they were all downright atrocious-looking to us after we broke up. But when we loved them, we loved everything about them, and they *appeared* better looking to us, even if no one else could see it.

I decided to listen to her and go out with Ryan again. He surprised me by taking me to dinner, an ice sculpture festival, a comedy show, and he was always the first to pull out his wallet.

On our first date he seemed so cheap and uninterested that his generosity made me think maybe I had misjudged him in more areas than just his appearance. With each date, I grew to like him more, and it was clear that he liked me, too. Even though I was hesitant at first to make our relationship official, gradually, it occurred to me that there might be a future with this guy.

The first time we had sex was on a lazy Sunday afternoon. It started as cuddling on Ryan's tired couch under a blanket, watching television. Soon enough, we turned to each other, grasped at buttons and zippers, and tried to not topple onto the floor. Then we relocated to his bedroom; clothes came off, a condom wrapper fell to the floor, and fumbling coitus took place for three whole minutes. There was no vocal indication that he was nearing the end. Instead, his face reddened, twisted, and contorted into something that was both so hideous and hilarious that I had to look away, and then it was over.

Oh my god, I thought, for all the lead-up, what a complete miss on the delivery.

Afterward, he pulled me into his body and kissed my forehead. "That was super awkward," he said.

I didn't know whether to feel relieved or offended. Instead, I pulled away a little and stared at him.

"It's never good the first time," he said. "I'm not a serial dater, but I know *that*."

I laughed, thinking he was right. Maybe there was potential for us after all.

The first time he met my friends, a group of us went out for drinks, and I quickly noticed that unless he was talking to me, he wasn't talking. Granted it was loud in the bar, but that didn't prevent anyone else from yelling over the music. Not initiating conversation was something I could understand, but he wasn't even reacting to others. When the rest of the table laughed, he just sat there, his disfigured expression unchanged, his eyes distant.

I was annoyed but decided to ignore it, assuming he was perhaps a little shy in groups. When we walked home that night, we were caught in heavy snowfall, stomping through deep drifts that filled the sidewalk. We shivered and complained and laughed the entire mile, snowflakes catching in my eyelashes, making my mascara run. I quickly forgot his lack of social participation at the bar. *Give this guy a break.* The words echoed in the folds of my mind whenever I started to feel uncertain or agitated around him.

In February, I invited Ryan to go with me to Chicago for a conference. I had been nominated for an award for my volunteer work advising and mentoring men in a fraternity, and the chapter was certain that I would win. We drove together in a snow storm most of the way,

Joe riding with us in the backseat, Austin, Mike, and the others in different cars spread out along the freeway.

At the celebration dinner, we found a table together in a large banquet hall packed with more than 450 college-age men dressed in suits. After receiving my award, twenty or so swarmed me with congratulatory hugs while Ryan stood off to the side or behind me, eying each of them suspiciously. I didn't care. This wasn't about him; it was about *them*: those young men for whom I had volunteered my time to guide their personal and professional development.

Joe was the reason I had started working with the fraternity in the first place. When he was a student and the chapter president, he approached me about the position, and then successfully convinced me to get involved, to overcome my negative perception of Greek life, especially fraternities. After he graduated and moved into my house, he stayed involved with the alumni organization which also received an award that weekend. I walked up to him after the dinner.

"This is because of you, you know," I said, then turned to receive a hug from another student before he could respond.

Later that night, Ryan and I gathered in a hotel suite with others to celebrate and spend time with friends who I didn't get to see often, because they lived out of state. Just two hours into the party, Ryan was pleading with me to leave. He claimed he was nervous about sharing space with so many people who were drinking. I encouraged him to go back to the room if he didn't want to stay, but he insisted that I go with him. It wasn't his nervousness talking; it was his libido. I delayed as long as possible and finally gave in because his complaining was making it difficult for me to enjoy myself.

Just as I was getting ready to leave, I saw Max—a young guy of maybe twenty and a member of a different chapter—wander out of the bathroom and lean against the edge of a bed. The red cup in his hand tipped slightly, and the beer hovered at the brim. He was struggling to keep himself upright while sitting on the corner of the mattress, his eyes red and narrow slits drooping on the front of his face. All around him, small groups of people huddled together, talking and laughing; I was the only one who noticed Max was struggling.

I approached him and put my palm on his shoulder to steady him while taking away the beer with my other hand.

"Max?" I said, and he looked at me without recognition, his eyes unable to focus. He accepted water from me, sipping it steadily and with tremendous focus. I talked to him, asking him where he was from, what his major was, how many siblings he had. My worry subsided a little after he started being responsive but didn't want to leave until it he was coherent. Ryan nudged me out the door anyway, ignoring my protests and pleas to stay.

Back in the hotel room, I raided the snack bar for carbs and settled on a bag of chips for Max before heading back out into the hall.

Ryan yelled, "Babe, that's not your responsibility!" just as the door closed behind me, and I was filled with fury at his lack of compassion. I walked Max to his room while he crunched the chips one at a time, quietly weeping that he didn't deserve for me to be so nice to him.

After closing our door behind me and securing the chain, I crawled into bed next to Ryan, fuming as he ignored me. I asked him how he could ever question that it was my "responsibility" to take care of someone who drank too much?

He put his face close to mine, the blue light from the alarm clock illuminating the room just enough for me to follow his misshapen lips as he said, "You're right. You have a big heart. And that's why I love you."

It was the first time he had said it. I responded by rolling away to answer the ringing phone.

"Austin needs you," Joe's voice was direct and deep on the other end of the line. "He's not doing so good."

There were four of them sharing a double room, Joe and Austin both tucked into one of the queen beds. I climbed between them and settled in under the covers, ignoring how Ryan might react to such a scene if he walked into the room at that moment.

Austin's disappointment at not winning a competitive award that he highly deserved, had finally sunk in after they spent a night out in Chicago celebrating the chapter's other successes. He didn't want to talk, but I knew that we didn't have to say anything.

I sat in that bed between the two of them until everyone in the room was asleep except Joe and me.

"I think I need to break up with Ryan," I said, adjusting the blankets stretched over my lap.

Joe nodded. "Yes, you do."

I turned to him surprised, though I shouldn't have been. He always knew before I did how it was all going to work out.

"You know this?"

He gave me that look of his that he gave me when I said something that underestimated him.

"Please," he smiled, and then his face shifted back to serious. "This is a lot for any guy to handle," he said in reference to the fraternity and the conference. "He can't handle you giving your time to so many other people. Most men can't."

"I'm going to be single forever," I said, and put my head on his shoulder.

"Maybe." Joe was never one to hesitate with the truth. "But would that be the worst thing?"

I sat back up and was quiet for a minute.

"I'm worried about Austin."

Joe nodded.

"I'm worried about you, too."

He didn't nod that time.

"You have darkness around you, Joe." I studied the hands in my lap. It didn't make sense to look at him because he wasn't going to return my gaze.

"I'll be all right."

I let the space of the room settle in around us. It didn't matter that we were packed in there with three others, or that Austin slept heavily next to me. "Am I a horrible person if I make Ryan drive us both all the way home tomorrow and then break up with him?"

"It would be worse if you broke up before we left, and then I have to sit in the back seat of your car while you two are in the front, *not* in a relationship. How awkward would that be?"

I wrapped my arms around his waist and squeezed, but I didn't let go because he hugged me back.

"What's going to happen to us?"

"Us?"

"You and I. Are we hopeless?"

The question hung in the air for a minute before I noticed Joe wipe his hand across his face to clear away stray tears. I felt gutted.

"*You're* not," he said. He stared hard at his hands before finally turning to me. "That award that you won? You earned that. Don't give me credit for that. Don't ever give anyone credit for something that is yours."

After returning to my hotel room and a sleeping Ryan, I stayed awake almost until dawn, replaying the scenes from the evening in my mind. Disappointment and regret filled the room around me as the minutes faded into hours. I wanted to celebrate. Ryan wanted to copulate. He didn't go to Chicago to support me; he went there under the guise that it would be some kind of romantic getaway for us, with no regard for my purpose for the weekend.

Ryan had been a different person in the beginning. Talkative. Inquisitive. Interested. Interesting. Everything between us had been on a steady incline until that December afternoon when our clothes had come off. Then it was officially the end of the relationship as I had known it. It didn't matter how much rolling around, hands under shirts, or lazy fumbling of belt buckles that had occurred up to that point. The closeness, the trust, the long-winded conversations, three-hour-long make out sessions, and intimacy in general quickly fell by the wayside after we got naked.

Our time spent together was just a preamble to sex. I connected the moments and thought of all the times he had pressured me to leave events early, pass up on one more drink, skip the movie on dinner and movie nights, just to get home sooner and shag. Our relationship became transactional. He always bought dinner, but he also always wanted sex. I wanted to like him. But I also wanted a relationship that didn't need sex to have substance, and I couldn't have that with Ryan. The more he wanted me, the more I lost interest.

After teaching an evening class the following Monday, I went over to his house, just like I had done all semester. He called the little restaurant on the corner and ordered dinner: A chicken pita wrap for himself and a Greek salad for me.

"No feta and esthra beeths," he said, and I cringed at his impediment. Everything about him now made me recoil.

We sat side-by-side on the couch in front of a rented movie, and I felt a growing sense of trepidation the closer it got to bedtime. He would want me to stay over just like I had always done. He looked over at me occasionally, but I wouldn't meet his gaze. I flinched when he shifted and moved too close to me. The room was exactly the same as it had been the first time I saw it, and the smell hadn't gotten any better. Although the windows were open and there was a light breeze circulating throughout the apartment, it felt even more confining than that first day when I had so much hope that he was something, someone, different. It was as though every nerve in my body was bursting through my skin, and I wanted to scream. This place, this relationship, had made me unrecognizable to myself.

At eleven o'clock, he turned off the television. I knew it was time.

"I'm tired," I said, and shuddered at the unoriginal statement women have used for decades to get out of sex. "I need a good night's sleep. In my own bed."

I knew that was the end, and maybe he knew it, too, but he didn't try to convince me to stay. It was well within my right to just walk out, but I also knew that I'd been unkind to Ryan. Rather than telling him about the things that bothered me, I just expected him to know what my expectations and boundaries were and respect them without me ever giving him a chance to do so.

The other commitments in my life took precedence over our relationship and there was no changing that. Our brief winter romance would never blossom into spring. I was a coward who was going to disappear on him without any explanation or closure. Driving home, I left behind four DVDs on his table, shampoo in the shower, and a small chunk of my dignity in his bed.

Chapter Eleven

Two days before Christmas I sat at the plaintiff's table, an accordion file containing spreadsheets of calculated expenses, unpaid bills, and old bank statements in front of me. Dave sat at the defendant's table holding an envelope stuffed with crumpled receipts.

I was dressed in a gray suit usually saved for job interviews. Dave's suit looked slightly faded from age, the pants too tight in the waist. Behind a tall oak judge's bench, sat the magistrate in a black robe, skimming the small claims paperwork I filed a month prior, one afternoon before going to Ryan's house for dinner and movie night. I felt slightly more nervous than expected, Dave had a look of annoyance on his face, and the magistrate was visibly impatient.

"Have you two talked at all?" The magistrate stared over his glasses and down at us.

Dave and I looked at each other and shook our heads. We hadn't spoken in more than a year, not since before I met Ryan. Our only recent communication had been an exchange of letters, mine asking for money, his attorney denying me money, and finally a process server delivering a notice that I was suing him to collect that money, a move that surprised him to anger. I knew that it would but felt warranted, finally strong enough to seek something that was rightfully mine and to serve justice on someone who had wronged me.

"I'm going to step out of the room for a few minutes," the magistrate said. "The two of you talk this through and decide if you can come to an agreement on your own."

I turned toward Dave, feeling momentarily optimistic we could reconcile ourselves financially. Maybe all we needed was for someone to tell us to do so.

Just as the door closed, Dave's eyes shifted in my direction.

"You're not getting a dime out me."

The fleeting hope in me deflated quickly. I realized he was exactly the same man who denied his responsibility to contribute to our joined household. The passage of time hadn't changed him; it hadn't compelled him to accept responsibility. I opened my mouth to say something, to explain, but there was no good place to start. He was so angry and full of spite that the Dave I remembered wasn't recognizable.

"When I moved out," he continued, "I thought we were good, that everything was settled."

Our final months together sped through my memory: a break up, his attempt to negotiate a reunion, my refusal, his insistence, my reasoning, his explanations, my impatience, him finally moving out, and me watching the moving van drive down the street, his key in my hand, and a sense of relief relaxing my body.

"By then I just wanted it to be over." I didn't have the gumption necessary to put up a fight, that any conflict with him would have put me right back to standing in front of Raul's closet while getting pelted with my own gifts to him.

"Why did you wait so long to do anything about it?"

Softening my voice, I said, "I knew you didn't have the money."

The truth was, I hadn't known my options, my rights, to collect what he owed me. Instead, that time had been used to see myself through the eyes of other men, to experience the aftermath and the struggle of what we could have been while searching for my own desires. Regardless of any of that, he was a grown man and there was nothing left for him to do but grow up.

He scoffed and curled his lips into a frown. "So you let a year go by and have my parents' house served at seven o'clock in the morning?"

I was tempted to look away but didn't want to appear fidgety or uncertain.

"It was the only address I had," I said. "I have no control over what time they show up with the paperwork."

He shook his head and looked away. His shoulders remained tense.

"You didn't pay a single bill for most of the year we lived together," I continued. "No one should have to support you."

"I have a pile of receipts here to show what I did pay for." He pointed to an envelope stuffed with bar tabs and miscellaneous trips to the grocery store, all of which he paid for with a credit card until he had no credit left.

I finally looked away. "I've been working three jobs to recover from the debt you left me with." It was taking a toll on me to work full-time and teach extra classes four nights a week, all in an effort to lower the balance on my own credit card month after month, the numbers barely shrinking. I was fed up and exhausted.

The magistrate returned to the courtroom.

"Well?" he asked. "What did you decide?"

Dave shrugged his shoulders to indicate we would have to proceed with the hearing.

After we took an oath to tell the truth, the whole truth, and nothing but the truth, it was my turn to present my case. I opened my folder, retrieved my spreadsheet, and reviewed the numbers. Unpaid rent. Ignored electricity bills. Funds borrowed and not repaid. The magistrate listened and jotted down notes, only interrupting to verify details or dollar amounts.

Mary Beth and my friend Leslie sat behind me in the courtroom, sworn in, too, and ready to testify, if necessary. They had both been there during the years I supported Dave, had heard his empty promises the money was coming: that it was just a matter of another week, or month, or sometime soon. I couldn't see them but could sense them silently cheering me on as I gave each detail with accuracy and specifics.

The only time I had ever been to court prior to the lawsuit was during my divorce hearing when John and I sat together and watched couple after couple stand at a podium and be pronounced ex-husband and ex-wife. If I was feeling anything then, it was impatience as we waited our turn and anticipation that we would be done soon so I could get to work before losing more pay. There was no case for us to present then. Instead, we were called to the front and waited as the magistrate reviewed the details of the paperwork: how we split belongings worth more than $250 which was easy. I wanted almost nothing, and John was the spender; he was the one with the expensive bike, guitar and amp, brand new laptop, and other playthings for grown-ups he insisted on buying. I didn't have anything like that.

To initiate the divorce, I had been the one to file, and he could never quite accept that he was listed as "defendant," as though I had attacked him with the paperwork and he had to justify his decision to marry me in the first place.

"How do we file together?" he had asked.

Of course he wouldn't know we couldn't because I had done the research. I had gone to the courthouse, paid for the packet, then paid again to file it. Because it was uncontested, and because we had no children or assets and no lawyers were involved, I wrote a check for $150 which secured a court date and a notarized signature to make the paperwork official.

"It cost you less to get divorced than it cost me to break my cell phone contract," my friend Victoria said to me while we walked laps around vacant downtown buildings during my lunch hour.

Despite my laughter, I had paid in other ways, like for my own wedding ring, an old-fashioned white gold and diamond setting I started to dislike by our third year together. I had paid for most of the wedding with some help from my parents, but none from him or his. Even after paying then, I still took care of Dave. I didn't want to think of the many times in between both relationships when I had paid in some way because of a man in my life.

By the end of the divorce hearing, the magistrate started calling me by my maiden name, a name I hadn't had in four years, a name I had missed. When we walked out of the courthouse that warm March afternoon, John had turned to me and asked, "How do we know we're not making a mistake?"

I didn't have an answer for him. I just knew.

When Dave presented his side in the small claims case, he spoke quickly, trying to talk his way out of responsibility through diversions: how he was able to successfully break the apartment's lease without penalty when I bought my house, how he had receipts—he held up the bulging envelope—of purchases he had made, items like Pepsi and toilet paper and shaving cream, all of which, he asserted, should absolve him of rent and utilities. The magistrate disregarded his argument, concluding all of those miscellaneous receipts Dave piled onto the table were just that: miscellaneous.

Then Dave produced a few utility bills for the times that he had made payments and insisted that the amount of that payment be removed from the grand total. There were a few gas bills and an electricity bill from our apartment, totaling just over $300.

The magistrate looked up from the notepad in front of him and down at me. "Do you agree?" he asked. "That you should be responsible for that amount?"

I had been paying careful attention. Dave either wasn't smart enough to realize the discrepancy or he was hoping that I wasn't. "I would agree that I'm responsible for half of that," I said. "Not all of it. What I'm asking for from him is half of the total expenses. He's asking for all of it."

Celebratory energy came from Mary Beth and Leslie as Dave

slouched in his chair and hunched his shoulders.

"Nice catch," Leslie told me later. "Your sister and I fist-bumped when you shot back with that one."

In the end, Dave and I were the only ones who had to testify. The magistrate had heard enough. After a recess to calculate the numbers, he ruled in my favor, awarding me just over $3,000.

Thirty days later, Dave appealed the decision. Another three weeks after that, I was back in court, this time scheduled to go before a judge whose decision was final.

The hearing was scheduled to start at 9 a.m. I arrived in the courtroom fifteen minutes early and so nervous, I was sweating through my suit. This was different than the hearing. This time, a judge would preside, and I had no idea what Dave was prepared to say.

At 9:20, the room started to fill up around me, and no Dave. No judge, either. It was the end of January, and the first snow storm of winter was making its way to the ground outside, delaying everything inside the courthouse.

At 9:21, Dave walked in and sat near the back. I was in the second row and just knowing he was behind me sent my nerves pulsating throughout my scalp. All of my documents were organized in a folder resting on my lap, including the verdict from our hearing with the magistrate a month prior. Leslie came with me again, but Mary Beth had to work. It didn't matter. I didn't need them there, but Leslie was the kind of person who liked to see things through to their end.

After the judge arrived, we watched a few cases go before us, and my nervousness grew with each one. Instead of standing before the judge, however, a clerk called us into a conference room, and once again, I was asked to tell the story.

Dave disputed the security deposit from the apartment and had found a few extra bills he wanted credit for toward the judgment. They were just statements, though, and he couldn't prove who paid them. Since I couldn't prove it either, the clerk gave Dave the benefit of the doubt. Dave tried, yet again, to claim the entertainment, groceries, household expenses, and—like the magistrate—the clerk dismissed it.

In the end there was still a discrepancy of $2,154.14. The clerk gave us the option to come to a settlement agreement in that room, or it would go before the judge and we wouldn't have any say in the decision. I was ready to settle. There was serenity in knowing that Dave would pay. The actual amount didn't really matter anymore. The principle was worth more than the dollar.

Dave whipped out his calculator, punched some numbers, and said, "I can pay you $150 a month for the next twelve months. That's $1,800."

I just looked at him.

The clerk jumped in and divided the discrepancy amount by twelve. It came out to just more than $177, so I compromised. I suggested rounding it to $175 a month, bringing the total to $2,100, free and clear.

Dave punched some more numbers. "How about $160?"

I looked at him. Hard. Sat up as tall as I could. Squared my shoulders. I was ready for that moment.

"One. Seventy. Five." He was wearing his about-to-argue-back face. I didn't budge. Not physically. Not numerically.

He looked away, and his shoulders slumped in defeat. "Fine," he said. "I just want this to be over."

Dave handed the first of twelve checks to the clerk as if something in him wouldn't allow him to hand it to me directly. I held the check in my hand and studied the familiar handwriting, the scribble I watched him write on the tab during our first date, writing that used to appear on love notes left in the morning early on in our relationship, cards for my birthday, and later on grocery shopping lists, documents of practicality and purpose. Four years later, and the handwriting was the same, though I wanted to believe some things about the man were different, but I couldn't hope that the experience had changed him. Some things were different about me, though, I was certain. Our similarities had no unit of measure as our differences were incalculable.

I returned to the courtroom, Dave's check securely tucked away in my wallet, and looked at Leslie.

"You ready to go?"

"It's over?" she asked. "What happened?"

"I'll tell you in the car. The snow's coming down pretty bad now. I think we should avoid the freeway."

*

I imagined it was like hearing the *pop* when bat connects with ball, but the ball pivots and spins and flies away from the outfield, into the stands, and straight at my head. Instead of sitting in the lower deck of the stadium on a sunny day, though, I was seated in the driver's seat negotiating with fresh snow as it fell to the ground and froze; and instead of a ball heading toward me, it was an oncoming car that spun around and slid toward my vehicle sideways, lining up to smash in my driver's side door, like one hand high-fiving the other.

For a moment, I saw the outcome of the impact, heard the crunch of car on car, and felt my body shoved up onto the center console as my side of the car formed an accordion into itself. I heard glass break, saw nothing but my hands shielding my face, and felt my body stiffen then collapse. Zapping me with cold air, the snow attacked me as it came in through the broken window. Shards of glass slipped out of my hair, and my legs twisted and got stuck under the steering wheel.

But the imagined impact only lasted a moment. Instead, I jerked the wheel to the right and my engine revved in defense as it pulled itself up onto the curb, narrowly escaping the accident. The car rolled along the grass, turned onto concrete, and came to a stop at the exit of a parking lot.

Leslie stopped talking mid-sentence when she saw the car coming at us.

"Whoa, nice driving," she exhaled. Neither of us realized we'd been holding our breaths.

I put the car in park, opened the door to climb out, and looked around, expecting to see destruction in my wake. Leslie walked the perimeter of the car to check for damage: a cracked bumper, broken axel, popped tire. But there was nothing, not even a scratched hubcap from hopping the curb.

Thirty feet away, the other car stopped at an angle straddling the two lanes and blocking traffic behind him.

The driver ran to me screaming, "Are you okay?" then threw his arms around my neck and hugged me.

"I thought I was going to die!" he said. "I thought you were going to die! Oh my god, I think I'm in shock!"

I hugged him back, trying to calm him down, and also trying incredibly hard to not laugh. I wasn't mad or panicked. More than anything, I was bewildered, still not entirely certain about what had just happened. All I knew was I had one thought before turning the wheel: *If he hits us, I'm the one who is going to die*, and then briefly, just briefly, hesitated before pulling the car out of harm's way.

"Are you okay to drive?" I asked him. "Do you want me to call someone for you?"

He pointed across the street to an apartment complex about half a block away. "I was almost home."

"You should probably move your car then. It's okay. Everything is okay."

He apologized again and ran off. Before he got in he turned back and yelled, "I promise I'll drive slower."

I caught Leslie's eye just before climbing back into the car and saw surprise as well as fear in them, and a little amazement that we had escaped the situation without even a scratched tire or a dinged bumper. Expecting to feel my knees shaking as I put my foot on the break to pull the car out of park, my legs were surprisingly still and my body calm.

"You know, the way that car was coming at you, you could have been really hurt," she said. "Maybe even killed."

I nodded.

"Are you freaking out right now?" She looked out the window and back to me. "If I were driving, I would be freaking out. I'm kind of freaking out anyway."

I smiled to let her know it was okay, but a tight smile was all I could muster.

Leslie continued talking, but I was no longer listening. I could hear the intonations of her voice, the highs and lows as she verbalized her way through the stress, but I couldn't make meaning out of her words.

The familiarity of driving suddenly seemed quite foreign to me. My hand reached for the ignition to start the car, only to find it was still running. I looked down at the console trying to remember how to shift the car out of park. Unable to focus on the mechanics of it all, I struggled to follow the basic steps to put the car back on the road and continue driving home.

I saw that car come toward us, watched the way it was lining up to slide right into me, ready to crush me under its weight and velocity. For the slightest of moments, I accepted the possibility of death. Every emotion within my range of capability piled onto itself and settled into my core. Everything shifted from white to clear, and I felt a tranquility come over me in a way I didn't recognize.

For a single moment, I gave in; I gave up. It wasn't until I considered the chance I would live, and would be left with a damaged vehicle, a damaged body, both of which would take time and money to recover, time and money I didn't want to spend on such an endeavor. So the options that remained were to allow death to make the decision, or lurch the car to the right and be saved.

"I can't believe you're so calm," Leslie said. "You seem completely unfazed, like you do this every day."

I turned on the wipers to clear the snow collecting on the windshield.

"I can't believe it either. I've always imagined how I would react if I was about to get into an accident like that, but it usually only got as far as me screaming and holding onto the wheel tighter."

"I've spun out before," she said. "But I've never had anyone spin out and almost crash into me."

I shifted the car into drive and pulled up a little to turn back onto the street.

"Hopefully, you never have to. Let's go home."

Chapter Twelve

"When you first meet a woman, you have a very narrow window," Drake paused and I could imagine him drawing a small box in the air with his fingertips. "It's tiny. Just big enough for you to put your hand through and touch her heart. Once you're there, though, the window gets bigger, and eventually you can climb through. But if you shove a bunch of stuff in there first, there's no room for you anymore, and she moves on to someone else."

We were on the phone for an hour, maybe longer. It was one of those conversations that started without reason and continued because a lack of purpose was easier than saying good-bye. Even though I listened and laughed, with him I fought feelings of overwhelming failure. Our back-and-forth time in River City had been going on for months, and—like our phone conversation—it had no purpose and no endpoint.

We didn't speak much anymore of that other girl, the one who claimed she had an abortion. I never believed she was actually pregnant though, at least not by him. There were too many variables, too many narrative threads: an ovarian cancer survivor, apparent ectopic pregnancy, rushed trips to the emergency room, an appointment scheduled, rescheduled, and rescheduled again around various mystery conditions and a road trip to a clinic that existed in Detroit, and only in Detroit.

"Happy not-a-father's day," I told him.

He counted me as two women, two proverbial notches on his belt, and he didn't count her at all. "That's how meaningless that was."

"No one on this phone is convinced by what you said," I responded.

"Well, good thing there's only two of us, and one of us is crazy."

It wasn't entirely clear which one of us he meant, and I didn't ask. Instead of offering an explanation, he extended an invitation. I wanted to see him, despite my initial resistance. Needing to make sense of us meant needing to ask him some difficult questions, so it didn't take long for him to convince me.

I went back to River City. It was a Friday. I had been home from work for just two hours before I got back in the car, an overnight bag in the trunk, and made the late-night, last-minute journey across the state to his childhood home. Arriving with a liter of Jack Daniels and a case of

Leinenkugel, I had an air of disregard for making any reasonable decisions.

Sitting on his bed, I leaned forward, holding the beer bottle close to my body, and stared intently at the computer screen. Drake was showing me graphics, typography he created. He'd gone away and emerged a designer. Or at least he would become one someday. He would design logos and print T-shirts, and sell them in a small store in a downtown shopping area that catered to tourists and teenagers.

"I just want to have a job where I can hang out and use my free time to go longboarding," he said.

I listened to him describe everything he showed me and remembered none of it. He had agreed to talk, to give meaning to the things between us that had created so much uncertainty for me. I didn't pressure him, though. He needed a drink first, maybe two, that telling the truth—even to me—required relaxation and self-coaxing.

Drake looked over at me as he made a point and could see it on my face that I wasn't listening. He switched out of the screen he was working on and scrolled through song lists before settling on Duran Duran, lowered the volume, then leaned back against his headboard, facing me.

I stared down at his comforter and found myself hesitatingly quiet. While raising a beer bottle to my lips, our eyes met.

"So," he said.

I smiled. "So."

"How do you want to start?"

I fidgeted with the blanket folds, shifting them into different peaks and valleys on the bed in front of me. "Why don't you start from the beginning?" I asked. "We've always been friends and always had this connection. But why did you reach out to me?"

He took another drink, a long one, the room deflating without his voice to keep it alive. "I was struggling," he started. "You know, I had these questions. Who am I? Where is my place? What does it mean to be a man in my family? I had an identity crisis. I was uncomfortable with who I was. My life was complete chaos, nothing was making sense, and nothing was making me happy. I reached out because I trusted you, and I was scared. I thought if there's any one person I can trust, she knows what I've been through, she wouldn't hurt me. And you lived up to that. You protected my skeletons, and I got through it."

I nodded. "I hope you feel like you can always trust me."

"Well, yeah," he said. "I still had to live the reality, but you helped me get rid of the pain. You pulled me out of my puddle of tears, and told me I know you're better, and you can do better. No one holds me accountable aside from myself, but you did." His voice dropped a flight of stairs, the laughter-like cadence leveling out during the free-fall. Neither one of us were accustomed to him being so forthcoming.

"Why not just leave it at that?" I asked, referring to our nights together. "It didn't have to go as far as it did."

His hands shook before a palm raked his fingers through his hair. "I realized what I've been doing with all these girls. I was sleeping with women to make myself feel like a man, thinking, that's what men do. Then I discovered that I could be selective. With you, I made that choice. I made that decision. I felt safe again, confident in myself, and back on track with my life." He paused and then smiled. With softness in his voice that I had never heard before he added, "That's a good memory."

Normally, I would dismiss him when he spoke in metaphors, when he would try out new words and new ideas on me, but that time, he seemed to mean what he said. I didn't know how to respond.

"You just stop and help and you say, 'You don't owe me anything.' You're not quid pro quo," he said. "I don't know anyone else like that; I don't know any women like you. You're just always there. Even when you're not, I know you will be."

He had done so much by saying so much. I had to give him something but didn't have the words the way he did.

"When you weren't there, I felt the absence of you." My voice was low, almost a whisper. That absence was a type of sadness that lived deep inside, taking up permanent residence far beyond any reachable place, but I didn't tell him that. I didn't want to treat our conversation like an open mic night of confessions. One person baring his soul was enough.

"You and I, we connected," he said. "We are connected. Like a brain wave."

"We are," I agreed. "We always have been. Since the very beginning there was something about us. Even other people could see it. People would ask me about you and how you were without knowing that I ever saw you. They just assumed that I did. Of course they assumed right, but it always surprised me."

He laughed his roaring laugh, deep and level and from his gut. "We do love you, Melissa, we all love you. And by we, I mean myself."

His love and my love were hardly the same. I nudged him away, trying to ignore his declaration but couldn't. Instead, I got us another drink, and returned to find he had gone back to his screens, back to his stories behind the images and the designs. I listened and encouraged. And finally, I accepted his invitation to join him in the shower. In the morning, I ran across the driveway in the rain, dawn just barely making an appearance, to kiss him one more time, not knowing then it would be the last time.

We were always apart more than we were together. And during that time, I imagined him immersed and focused, hunched over a sketchpad. I saw him crossing campus with a backpack, in class, with friends. He was shielded, reclusive, the depths of himself kept hidden. Even when we talked on the phone for hours—typically three at minimum—running out of time before running out of topics. Even when I sent him packages in the mail— homemade gifts and cookies one year, a mini-fridge the next—to make him happy, to let him know that he meant something to someone, even if that someone was me.

Another fall faded into another winter. Snow blanketed River City. During another visit, he turned to me on a torturously cold February evening and said, "Never waste a cigarette, booze, or the company of a good woman."

In the morning, snowflakes the size of quarters fell and collected on the grass. I expected them to make the cling-cling-cling sound of slot machines, but they were silent.

My affection, although distant, was unconditional. But my longevity was not. He didn't want any more than what we had. I needed more than he was able to give. That impasse was where it ended. He groaned and pouted and claimed that he was, as he put it, a sore loser. But he didn't compromise, he didn't beg, and I didn't expect him to.

He was the kind of man I wanted to love. Or maybe he was the kind of man I wanted to love me. He held me to a certain level of admiration that was unmatched by anyone else. I saw him a way no one else did, from the inside out. To me, he was elusive comfort, a connected persona, albeit a transitory experience. To him, I was a lady and a concubine. To each other, we were just each other. I was trouble. He would always be River City, but not the one I had been searching for. Not anymore.

Chapter Thirteen

"You look very nice this evening," Jason said to me from across the restaurant table.

Donning straightened hair and fresh makeup, I looked the best I could for a date that was scheduled at the end of a long day of teaching.

"Thank you."

"You're welcome." He tapped his hands on the tabletop, and I noticed how small they were, the fingers short and thin like a child's.

We were set up, and I was okay with that. At work one evening, my friend Linda said, "My nephew might be the guy for you. He's so funny." Then I heard story after story of family gatherings where Jason's humor was the center of the party, where his jokes would take over the crowd and all would be roaring in laughter as plates of food were passed around, and small children zig-zagged throughout the many chairs, coffee tables, and piles of gifts splayed about.

I was letting go of Drake and had started to consider the possibility of not seeking out love any longer, of not looking for a man who could be my River City. But Jason seemed like a different kind of man, and I needed to break the pattern.

"I told him about you," Linda said one afternoon while I hovered at the desk where she answered phones and greeted campus visitors. "I may have shown him a picture, too," she chuckled.

"Linda!" I gave her a look of embarrassment, though flattered. We had known each other for about a year, and to be invited to date someone in her family meant a lot to me.

She asked if she could give him my number, and he contacted me that night. A few days later, Jason and I met for dinner at a restaurant with giant cutouts of lobsters and pictures of fishing boats decorating the plank wood walls, followed by amateur night at a comedy club.

When he dropped me off at my car, he leaned over and kissed me, a gentle kiss with assertive confidence. From my backseat, I retrieved a fleece blanket that I had made for him bearing the logo of his favorite sports team. It wasn't like me to give a gift to someone I had just met, but our conversations leading up to our first date and Linda's descriptions of Jason, compelled me to do something nice and unexpected. Maybe if I changed myself, I would change the kind of man in my life, too.

"Wow," he said, running his fingers over the material. "This is beautiful."

I waved my hand and looked to the ground. "It's nothing. I just felt like making you something."

"You're beautiful," he said, and kissed me again.

We moved quickly. Maybe it was because we were both in our thirties and had openly declared that we were ready to settle down. After a week, he pushed to stay the night, though I resisted for another week after that. We weren't immediately intimate; we didn't need to be. The proximity of our mature bodies to one another, our breathing matched in exhale as we slept, was enough to make us both comfortable.

Once he started sleeping at my house, he never stopped, though he didn't actually move in; he didn't have a key of his own. We didn't talk much about the next step, only about the ultimate goal: Jason and I both wanted to get married. We probably wanted to get married to each other

Three weeks after our first date over salmon risotto and popcorn shrimp, he took his hands and put both through my hair, fingers spread wide and combing along my scalp. He then pressed his mouth against my cheek and kissed me before whispering, "I love you, baby."

I thought it came too soon. But it felt good to be loved. It felt good to hear that somebody loved me, that I was deserving of love, because I hadn't had it, not in the way that I wanted, not in a long time.

"How do you know?"

"I just do," he said. "You're the best part of my day." His words felt good to hear, though maybe good for the wrong reason, a reason I hadn't yet come to realize.

Later that night, he stroked my cheek and said, "Please don't flirt with other guys in front of me."

The request came out of a silent room around us. My body stiffened. There was a tug at the base of my skull, an alarming sense of something that I couldn't name, but I knew it was wrong. I took a moment and tried to process what he had said. A lot of my friends were men, which he knew. I had Joe, a male roommate, who he had met. There was Glen, a male friend with a long history of being a confidante and only a friend, who Jason had met and even liked. And so I asked him. Where had that come from? Why would he say that?

No matter how I phrased my questions, all he could say was, "It's just my past. It's just my past. I don't know. It's just my past. I don't know."

I would hear "I don't know" a lot, would hear it whenever he was angry with me because he could never explain why. Maybe I didn't have the right words to ask. Maybe there were no right words to say.

*

Joe handed me a stack of twenties. "Here's November rent," he said. "And also my notice that I'll be moving out December first."

I knew he had been unhappy. It hadn't been just the two of us in quite some time, as I rented out the second bedroom for a while, and then Jason was at the house almost every night. It was busy, it was noisy, and it was no place for an introspective introvert like Joe.

Nevertheless, I didn't know how to react to his announcement. "Aren't you going to miss your dog?" I asked. Duke rested in the corner, chewing on a raw hide.

Joe slumped to a seated position on the kitchen floor, ready to hash it out. "Yeah," he said. "And you." Then he told me about his new apartment: a third-story walk-up with more space than he needed and a hefty price tag. "I need to know that I can do this on my own."

"This feels like a break-up," I said. "I feel like I'm getting dumped." Even though I could sense it was coming, I still didn't know how to react except to pretend to be supportive and hope it turned into the truth. For once, I was the one who didn't want to talk. I went upstairs to my room and left him behind on the cool tile.

"I have such mixed feelings," he said the next day. "I think that living alone is something I should experience, but I also don't want to leave you."

"Don't stay because you think I need you. Stay because I want you to."

"I know," he said.

In the end, he didn't stay. I couldn't have both a Jason and a Joe.

Shortly after Joe moved out, Jason and I huddled together under blankets while watching television in a dark bedroom, the house empty and quiet around us.

I turned to Jason. "Do hear that?"

He looked at me and shook his head. "What?"

"That noise."

"It's probably outside." He burrowed down under the blankets and got comfortable. My bedroom window was right above the neighbor's driveway, so it wasn't an unfair assumption. The noise wasn't coming from the neighbors, though.

"No." I muted the TV. "Listen."

He picked his head up off the pillow and stared at me.

"It sounds like people talking in the living room, maybe the kitchen. Doesn't it?" I shifted a little toward the door. A mumbling noise made its way up through the floor boards, so distinctive that it couldn't be ignored.

There was someone in my house. Of that, I could be certain.

"I'm going to see what it is." I climbed out of bed and looked around my room, for what, though, I didn't know. There wasn't a baseball bat or knife or gun, despite Glen's relentless encouragement for something to defend myself with. I headed toward the stairs empty-handed.

"Well, I'm coming with you," Jason said, following close behind me, though I wasn't sure how much use he would be. He was two inches shorter and at least forty pounds lighter than I was. Safety in numbers, I guessed.

I made my way down the stairs and opened the door. It wasn't voices, but music.

"It's the Indigo Girls," I laughed. "But where is it coming from?" I turned the corner and walked into the living room to find one of my cats lying on the power button of my docked iPod. The hair on the back of my neck and arms settled as Jason scoffed and stomped up the stairs.

"Phantom," I said to the cat and shooed him away. "You're really living up to your name."

After turning the power off, I closed the front room curtains, and then checked the locks on the doors, just in case. By the time I got back upstairs, Jason was already asleep and didn't notice me crawling in next to him.

I thought of the night I slept on the floor to keep Tony from choking in his sleep, and how Joe watched over us for hours, even though he was tired and had to work in the morning. Joe would have checked windows and locks and listened to me chatter about what it really meant to have any security. He wouldn't have returned to his bedroom until he knew I wasn't afraid anymore, that my worries had calmed down, and we could both go to sleep without concern.

Joe and I had one last project together for the fraternity before I stepped down from my volunteer position. We camped out in the woods in Ohio with 180 college-age men as volunteers for EDGE—a leadership development program.

With over a year of living together, it truly felt like we had a solid relationship where we could work among each other without fumbling, anticipating how the other would move and turn. I knew it was the last time we would be together leading anything that mattered, or be a part of something bigger than our collective selves.

Back in Michigan, Jason spent the weekend sleeping on his parents' couch and Michelle spent the weekend with Duke. We had left behind the ones who loved us so we could serve as role models and guides for others. We were a team.

Throughout the weekend, we saved seats for each other at meal times. Whenever I needed help setting up for the next event, he was at my elbow offering his assistance. Joe was my go-to technical expert. He brought participant issues to my attention so we could resolve them together. *Together.* Together, we had built a sharper EDGE.

The last event of the weekend took place in the mess hall where all of the participants stood in one large circle and stepped forward when statements that applied to them were read aloud.

Cross the line if you've cried in the past month.
Cross the line if you've been hurt by someone you love.
Cross the line if you've hurt someone you love.
Cross the line if you've ever been arrested.
Cross the line if . . .

Joe stood next to me, and it took everything in me to not reach out and squeeze his hand when we stepped forward and revealed new things to the group, some to each other. I would never again be that close to him physically or emotionally. Together we had crossed our own line, and for us, there was no stepping back.

I returned to Michigan, and Jason welcomed me home with a small box tied with a ribbon.

"Uh-oh," Jason said, as he pulled it out of his pocket. "What could this be?"

I was in bed reading a book, propped up on my side to see the pages. *It's too soon*, I thought. *Not yet. Please, not yet.*

"It's not my birthday," I said, a little too upbeat for my anticipation to be convincing. "What's this for?"

He handed it to me and grinned, his smile extended so big that lips peeled back from his gums to reveal a dark brown spot at the root of one of his front teeth, a dark spot I hadn't noticed until that very moment. It was the first time I thought maybe he wasn't attractive; maybe I wasn't attracted to him.

I sat up in bed and opened the box. Inside, at the end of a platinum chain, was a black and white diamond pendant. The light from overhead reflected off the stones as the pendant rested in my outstretched palm.

It was beautiful. Beautiful and undeserved. But I didn't tell him that. Instead I smiled, thanked him, leaned forward and kissed him. In that moment, I felt relieved and grateful I had found a man who thought of me for no reason, a man who was caring, a man who expressed his love with abandon. I had found a different kind of man. Maybe he was the one I had been looking for all along. I loved him; I could love him.

*

Jason's anger came on suddenly, and yet I think maybe it had always been there. There were signs so early on, the night he declared his love, the night he held me close and begged me to never flirt with other men, to never hurt him. I never would, I promised.

Except that I did.

One morning I came out of the bathroom after taking a shower. I was in the middle of wrapping a towel around my head when he held up my cell phone and said, "We need to talk. Who is Drake?"

It was late morning. He hadn't been drinking then. Something else had compelled him to plick my phone up off the nightstand and scroll through years' worth of text messages exchanged with any male he hadn't met and dig deep into the history, deep into the relationship, until he found something he didn't like.

He scrolled through my life with Joe, my friendship with Glen, students inquiring about homework assignments, college talk with my brother (until he realized it was my brother), until he got to Drake. Then he read and read and read, then asked questions, even though he wouldn't listen to the answers. Every answer turned into a new question where he tried to twist my truth into something it wasn't.

"I told you the worst thing you could ever do was cheat on me," he said.

Cheat? *Cheat?* Why? Because I had continued to talk to Drake long after our days in River City had ended? Because I had flirted a little sometimes? Had I reminisced with him too much about our connections that had shaped me? Cheat? Really?

"That's cheating to me," Jason said. "You talked to another man about sex. You kept him in your life. It was just a matter of time before you slept with him."

Just like that, my mind wasn't there anymore. My mind was back in Las Cruces, back in Raul's apartment, back in front of the closet packing my clothes, back to crying quiet tears because I couldn't defend myself against the words he said. I was back there discovering those naked pictures, I was the person who would search through someone's email, and I wondered, *Did I make Jason feel the same way Raul made me feel?*

No, I decided. He came to this feeling all on his own. This scowling person slouched on my bed was the cause of his own anger.

I tried anyway to talk to him but couldn't without his participation. Finally, he left and later, my phone exploded with text messages passing off accusations as questions.

"Either we talk in person," I finally told him, "or we don't talk at all."

Soon after, I realized Jason was a living, breathing phantom, complete with half his face, half his soul, hidden by a mask. It was evil hiding evil, breeding deeper evil. My instincts in reading others were challenged by people who lied to me, who deceived me, who convinced me that I must be mistaken. Jason was one of those people.

He said "I love you" with his gifts and "I hate you" with his words. When he was angry, his voice was strong, the words stunted and punctuated, the thoughts sharp and juvenile. His motives were unclear. I could just recall times where he looked at me with unequivocal hatred.

When the anger subsided, and it always did, the pleading began. He missed me and loved me. He blamed me. He was sorry he blamed me. It was the same ingredients trying to produce a different concoction each time.

I forgave him because it was Christmas, and I was alone. My sister announced her engagement and small wedding just before the holiday. I wanted him there. My parents came to town for the wedding and sat across from us at the small dinner at an Italian restaurant, a private affair where we dined among strangers, patrons who saw the balloons and the cake table and applauded my married sister when she arrived in her white gown, making her way between tables one step ahead of her new husband. She was all smiles that day, and she deserved to be.

Madison sat next to me at the end of the table, and I focused my attention on her, my niece who was celebrating a birthday in a month. She grinned at me, the splash of freckles across her nose crinkling as her smile widened, and I turned to Jason to share that moment with someone else. He put an arm around my shoulder and hugged me tightly, understanding the magic of that child. Those were moments I loved him the most.

I dished a spoonful of cheese ravioli onto Madison's plate and scooted her chair in closer to the table so she could reach it. Her process was methodical. She pierced each piece, opened her mouth wide and popped it in, chewing and smiling at me when I offered to order her a refill on her Sprite.

When it was time to leave, I slung Madison's backpack onto my shoulder, the one she had packed to spend the night at my house. I twirled her by the hand to make the skirt float before zipping up her coat.

Jason took the backpack from me after it slipped from my shoulder. I didn't have to ask him to do things; I didn't have to ask for his help. Earlier that evening he had shoveled the driveway for me, wearing my purple coat and snow boots just to give the neighbors something to wonder about. He helped me because I needed it, and when I needed it, without asking him. I wondered if he could easily fall into the domestic life of housework and maintenance and maybe even childcare. Maybe he was a different kind of man.

When we stepped outside the restaurant, the wind buried its claws into our exposed skin. Madison reached her two hands into the air, one for me and one for Jason, and we walked to the car while she chattered a child's story.

My parents came to visit the next day, and we gathered in front of the television to enjoy snacks, open gifts, and watch football. Jason drank Heineken, one after the other, the empty bottles lined up on the counter. Nobody seemed to care, but nobody accepted my offer for a beer or a glass of wine, either.

There was something off-putting about it, even though my family customarily drank at get-togethers, sometimes to excess. Moving throughout the house, I cleared plates and stacked dishes, going in and out of conversations. He was making a good impression as he expressed support for my parents' favorite team, even though I knew it wasn't his since the logo on their team's helmet didn't match the one on the blanket I gave him after our first date.

My parents told me later that they thought he was fake, and on so many levels, they were right. Jason could be two kinds of people when he drank. He was boisterous, outgoing, daring, something to laugh at. His punchlines were abrasive, never rude or off-color, just more exaggerated than necessary, forced and begging for a chuckle. Sometimes his antics went beyond the slingshots of jokes, though I often didn't see them in person. Instead, he showed me videos of him captured at parties, like the one where he was dressed in a red and white costume and flailed about while the crowd chanted, "Go Santa! Go Santa!" until he picked up a pool stick and tried to break it over his head. Instead of breaking, it sent him crumbling to the floor, dizzy and bleeding.

New Year's Eve. My mouth was tangy, the cocktail fresh and heavy on my tongue. I had lost count of my refills, succumbing to the encouragement to have another, have another, have another.

It had been his idea. "Let's get drunk and watch the ball drop."

We both knew we didn't want to go to a party. So when he suggested a night in, I agreed. We were fragile, having just come off of a ruinous argument a week prior, a fight so fierce that I almost spent my Christmas Eve eating cheesy potatoes and green bean casserole at Glen's mother's house, just so I wouldn't be alone. With just hours to spare, though, Jason had come around, had apologized, brought forth expensive gifts— a watch, black diamond earrings to match the diamond necklace he had given me months earlier, two Coach purses because he couldn't choose one that he thought I would like better—and had them each wrapped with thick, shiny paper and a bow. For one week, we loved each other again. One week.

Then on New Year's Eve, Jason's thick eye lashes slouched over his pupils, he yanked my hair hard to get my attention, and spat, "I bet you've had a threesome with two guys. Haven't you?"

There it was. Jason's worst fear and the most insulting of his assumptions.

Maybe I could make light of it.

"Not yet," I said. "Why? Did you have someone in mind?" I forced a giggle and smile.

He sneered. "You're just a slut. A bipolar slut."

I shut him out at that moment. He tried to bait me with those words, bait me into reacting. Would I cry? Become angry? Beg him to take it back? Call him names in return?

No. I didn't do any of those things. Instead, I stared straight ahead at the television, at the people hollering and cheering in Times Square, wearing crowns and hats to celebrate the beginning of another year. Jason stared at me while I watched them, taunting me to react. I didn't want to be on that couch with him the following year.

In an effort to diffuse his anger, I went upstairs, grabbed a book off my shelf, and pretended to read. I scanned over black lettering on graying pages but couldn't process their meaning. My mind was too preoccupied with processing *his* meaning. He came up from the basement, moved around on the other side of the wall, and lingered in the doorway, looking at me but not saying anything.

Keeping my gaze on the book, I ignored him. It was no use fighting with someone who didn't see me as worth fighting for. I wasn't going to ask him to justify his name-calling, his pigeon-holing, his dismissing me as someone beneath him.

He moved out of the room. I heard the bedroom door open, then slam shut, and the sounds of his heavy footsteps reverberated in the wall between us as he stomped up the stairs. In the living room I waited with the book in my lap.

When he had been quiet for a few minutes, I went upstairs and found him passed out in my bed, a bottle of cranberry juice and vodka on the floor next to him.

I didn't want to be in the house with him, so I called Michelle and asked her to come pick me up. Sitting on the front porch in the cold, I waited for her to arrive, afraid he would wake up and try to stop me from leaving.

When I returned home the next morning, Jason was gone. He took with him all of his belongings, every last thing, along with my bottle of Grey Goose vodka that was a birthday present from Joe.

*

I wasn't hungry but agreed to walk across the parking lot to the

Melissa Grunow

Coney Island where we would be obligated to order something in exchange for a quiet place to talk. It was the end of my first day back to work after the New Year; it had been a week since I had seen him, a week since he had shown me just how mean he could be.

Jason sat across from me, calm and relaxed, both arms resting on the table, his body open, just as he had been on our first date.

I leaned back in the booth and felt the cushioned plastic press up against my sweater.

"So, let's talk."

"Okay." He nodded with his whole body. For him, it was as though nothing had happened between us. He tried to convince me that he was sorry again and even said he signed up for classes to help with his self-confidence and therapy was the next step. Jason reached for my hand and tickled my palm with the tips of his fingers, a gesture so subtle and convincingly sweet, he must have believed it was the truth.

"You can't say things like that to me," I said. "You can't talk to me like that. I don't deserve that."

"It's just my past," he said. "I have all these fears."

"I will be a part of your past, too, if you speak like that to me again." I didn't recognize my own assertiveness. His face was so open and relaxed, that I couldn't help but to give him ultimatums. "Not even as a joke, not even sarcasm." I was firm on that point.

His hands raised in a gesture of surrender. "I will probably die as a result of being sarcastic to the wrong person at the wrong time." He had that same punchiness in his voice as he chuckled.

I glanced at my wrist, at the watch he gave me for Christmas. It was time to go. Teach a class, attend a meeting, see a friend. It didn't matter. We held hands as he walked me back to my car, but my desire for him was gone. I allowed him to kiss me good-bye and passively agreed to have dinner with him that Friday. Then I kissed his cheek, letting my lips linger until he opened his eyes, and I felt his lashes graze my forehead.

Before driving away, I looked at him one last time. There he stood in his pressed black pants, blue button-down shirt, tie, combed hair, shined shoes, and sleek pea coat. He looked uncharacteristically tall and would have cast a long shadow if there had been any sun.

We never saw each other again after that. I continued to wear the watch. The day and date weren't set correctly, and I never learned how to change them.

114

Part III
Surfacing

Chapter Fourteen

My return to New Mexico after a seven-year hiatus was a slap of familiarity as I sat in the passenger seat and headed south on I-25 toward Truth or Consequences. Unlike every other place in my world, New Mexico had remained unchanged to me, the freeway the only sign of civilization for miles between exits.

I didn't know until I got there that New Mexico would be on fire. The Silver Fire near Kingston had started weeks prior when lightning struck the dry ground. The sparks spread easily, the fire licking its way through 80,000 acres of the Gila National Forest. It continued to spread, threatening and devouring small towns in its way. They were towns where people had lived their entire lives on ranches or running general stores or museums, towns where the houses people abandoned were their only concept of home, towns with populations of less than a hundred, some less than twenty. They were quickly devoured by the fire and easily forgotten.

Still more than thirty miles away from Truth or Consequences, the fire presented a hovering threat as it covered the horizon with thick, dark smoke. The burning-earth smell filled the air, and ash drifted down from the sky like snow, a lingering reminder that the fire was ever-present, destructible, and menacing. It spread more and more each day, covering thousands of acres with only twenty percent containment.

When I arrived at the Starry Night residency compound, I was already out of place in jeans and a cardigan that draped over a drab T-shirt. The other artists were a poet, a visual artist, and the program manager, who was also a painter. I barely nodded a smiling hello before stumbling into my studio apartment, locked the door behind me, and slept until the next morning, the window A/C unit on full blast and unable to get my body temperature under control.

The first year I lived in New Mexico during graduate school, I cried nearly every day in the summer because of the heat. Maybe I had made a mistake going back there. Maybe the bits of notes and incomplete files of writing ideas would never become manuscripts because the heat, the memories too stifling.

It wasn't until the next morning after the night sky cooled the air that I was finally able to acclimate to the temperature. I emerged from my room and took up post in the tiny courtyard, settling into a patio chair with a book and waiting for the inspiration to come. Instead, I spent most of the time squinting at reflective pages, longing for a stronger Wi-Fi signal for my untouched laptop, and making small talk with the others as they passed by to their apartments. So early in my residency, and I felt like the odd one out, the introverted loner who was only getting more socially awkward the harder I tried to connect with others.

In the evening, I walked along the mountain foothills in the desert with the rest of the group, wishing I'd had changed out of my flip-flops and into closed-toe shoes before we left the compound. There were seven of us, some artists and some friends of artists, all strangers to me: people who I didn't know twenty-four hours prior, whose names I was still learning.

We stayed on a path the width of a one-lane dirt road. Tumble weeds and prickly pear cacti stood quietly around us, deeply rooted in the ground or growing out of the side of the foothill. If we listened, we could hear the movement of the Rio Grande flowing just on the other side of the brush.

Living in the desert was like living in stopped time. The plants that survived best were those which could survive without water and had found ways to defy nature. As a result, they were highly defensive, producing thorns—sometimes as long and as thick as toothpicks—to warn hikers and critters alike to stay away. I kept to the center of the path to protect my exposed toes from any of those desert threats.

While we walked along the base of the Turtleback Mountain foothills, Jada came across an animal skull, and with a smile on her face, pulled it from the brush.

She shook it out a little. "I hope there are no spiders in here," she said, and carried it the rest of the evening, with plans to bleach it and take it back to North Carolina at the end of her residency.

"Maybe it's a dog," Dafna guessed, noting its wide circular eyes and large snout, though other speculations named a fox, perhaps a coyote.

"I feel kind of strange knowing this might be a dog head," Jada said to me. A fox or a coyote skull found in the desert and proudly displayed on a shelf was a relic of the southwest. A dog head, though, would draw doubtful curiosity at best.

The sun was moving west as we continued to walk. I looked over my shoulder at the distance we covered. Maybe we went too far, I thought, but didn't speak up. We stepped over a cable suspended between two poles bearing a sign that read, "Private Property. No Trespassing," and kept walking.

Our group gathered in the ruins of a decommissioned silo, where nothing remained except piles of rocks, broken cinderblocks, and old grates, all contained within a short concrete wall decorated with graffiti. When I stood near a metal structure in the center, my voice bounced throughout the remains of the building, echoing in stereo. There were remnants of memories there, but they kept their secrets. We would never know what that building was for or why or when it was destroyed. There was only blight left behind, a rubble of wonder.

Dafna joined the two guys along the riverbank as they tried to skip stones into the water. They chattered about technique, how to hold the stone, how to release it, how to balance speed and angle. I stayed back, knowing I couldn't get the stones to skip—spending weekends on a Michigan lake as a child taught me that—but I also didn't feel right about sending something into the water that didn't belong there, of displacing the rocks from the shoreline. How long had they worked with the current to find themselves on the bank just to feel the heat of the desert sun? It felt unfair to me to disrupt their journey.

The sky was nearly dark. We decided to head back to the compound, and I stayed centered on the road out fear of rattlesnakes or other wildlife defending their territory. We came around a bend and walked toward the neighborhood. It was so dark I found myself squinting to see the ground in front of me, and I had to force myself to relax my eyes to ward off a headache that was already taunting me because of the heat.

Up ahead we saw the outline of a person walking toward us. I felt my body stiffen and fell one step behind Jada and Blake. We got closer and saw that it was an old woman out for an evening stroll, crouched forward as she made her way down the path.

"It's so nice to see other people out here," she said while passing us.

I relaxed my body as Blake's feet scuffled against the gravel.

"Does that freak you out to see someone walking toward you in the dark, or is it just me?" he asked.

Jada chuckled and made a reassuring joke that the old woman was probably non-threatening, and I muttered in agreement though didn't actually agree. I didn't speak of the impending fear I felt with each new experience, with every unfamiliar interaction. Jason's words were always in my memory, twisting and churning, challenging me each time I interacted with others. Instead, I quickened my step to fall in line with them again and kept walking toward the street lights and houses, the mountain at my back.

The next morning, it was finally time to start writing, but I already felt confined by my room. The thick cinderblock walls prevented the Wi-Fi signal from making its way down to my apartment. Opening the windows would just let in the dust and heat, but leaving them closed kept me too closed off, too. I went to Truth or Consequences to get away but didn't want to be entirely isolated.

After loading up my backpack, I walked into town to a little place called the Passion Pie Café. Monica, the owner of the retreat center, and Megan, her manager, had both assured me that it was the kind of coffee house where I could set up shop for the day, sip a beverage, nibble a scone, and write without any interruptions. It was exactly the kind of place I needed.

The bell jingled as I stepped in through the front door. The patrons' eyes settled on me and quickly determined I didn't belong there, for in a small town, all the outsiders were quickly realized and sized up. I ignored the stares and instead found a seat at an empty table in the corner near an outlet and the front window.

It was empty, I quickly discovered, because the heat from the unrelenting sun poured a glare over everything it could touch inside the café, including my table, chair, and the small space around me. I welcomed the brightness, though not the heat. If I could acclimate to the lone, oscillating A/C unit near the counter that just barely stretched to my corner, then I would have the space and time I needed to focus. I ordered a coffee and a muffin then settle into my chair. Six hours later when they prepared to close for the day, I had twenty new pages drafted and a renewed sense of purpose.

I went to the Passion Pie every day of my residency. Each day I woke up early before the others in the retreat center, walked the two miles to the café, and stayed there until they closed in the mid-afternoon. Then I walked back to my apartment, laid across the hot sheets, and slept. At night, sometimes I joined the others for dinner at a restaurant in town or a few drinks and free pool at a bar, but not always. I didn't want late-night raucousness to interfere with my day-time productivity. The purpose of my time in New Mexico wasn't to drink, and I was afraid if I started, if I got to that right level of drunk, that I wouldn't stop, and my two weeks away would be wasted.

The first week of my residency quickly spilled into the second. On Monday morning, I found myself again at the Passion Pie, an empty coffee cup next to me, rereading what I had written the week prior, skipping from document to Internet, unable in any way to get focused.

A man leaned over from the next table and asked, "Are you a writer? I'm a poet."

I had seen him there before. He showed up each day with a messenger bag and unloaded notebooks, a dictionary, thesaurus, a few copies of his own self-published books, and a small pile of others' books that he skimmed for inspiration. After settling in with a coffee or an iced tea, he slapped on headphones and waited for the poems to come. His routine was eerily similar to my own.

"I often write poems about women with tattoos on their arms." He nodded to the collage of flowers that spanned from just below my collarbone to just above my elbow. "I'd like to write a poem about yours."

I was not often receptive to conversations with strangers. Stan, however, caught me on a day where I was a little more open to the world I inhabited. He picked up his cell phone and scrolled through some pictures of tattoos on other women, tattoos of all designs, all sizes, and I was certain, all with different stories.

"Okay," I said. "Why not?"

He pulled out a piece of paper to take notes while I explained the entire design was a cover-up of my first tattoo, a rough rendition of a tiger head and a gift from Mark, my first ex-boyfriend. The tattoo, like the relationship, had become inconvenient and then meaningless. Within time, it no longer suited me or my personality. It had to go.

The new tattoo had three flowers, each representing a foreign country I had visited: the sunflower for my tour of Italy, a red hibiscus for my volunteer work in Haiti, and a lotus flower for the month I spent teaching English in China. There was also a train bell buried amongst the petals. My house was near busy tracks where passenger and cargo trains alike passed through town at all hours of the day and night. While some people may have found the train whistle to be a disruption, I saw it as a symbolic reminder that no matter what happened in life, I just had to keep going, and so that's what the bell represented.

Stan smiled as he took notes, asked a few clarification questions, then turned back around in his seat and started to write. I learned later that Stan's wife died in 2011, and her passing opened a spigot for poetry in her absence. A retired Naval Officer and pilot of carrier jet aircrafts, Stan lived with his cat and spent his days in coffee shops and bookstores in Truth or Consequences writing poems to pass the time.

I had just started to write notes for a new essay when Stan showed me his poem. It was a sestina that was confined by the line structure and word repetitions of the form, but he tried to make it narrative. The story wasn't entirely accurate, but I didn't correct him. I could appreciate the poem for the effort, for the art.

In the poem, he presented me more as an action, rather than a person, a verb instead of a noun. He personified adventure and gave her my name, my tattoos, my red hair. She was a moving locomotive, a passport stamp junkie who was fearless and bound for something predetermined. In reality, I was cautious, reserved, hesitant. My actual experiences had not felt so ambitious.

Smiling politely, I told him that I loved it. "It's not easy to tell someone else's story," I mused.

As I walked home after the Passion Pie closed down for the day, the sky darkened and reshaped its smoke cloud, negotiating with the sun, sometimes winning, sometimes losing. I stopped on the sidewalk and took in the smoke, the ash, as my lungs fought for clean air.

Every building, every vehicle along my path had a layer of soot. Nature shoved demise in our faces, getting so close we couldn't see beyond the remnants of its destruction, couldn't breathe without ingesting death. I thought of Stan's poem and the story he tried to tell. How different would it be for me to tell my own story? What would that story look like, and how would I fit into it? I had spent so much time already living for love—or the hope of love—pursuing my version of something that I called River City, something I wanted so badly, yet couldn't define for myself or anyone else. I was always seeking River City; I just never seemed to realize it.

It wasn't quite dusk yet, but there was darkness on the horizon. Jada drove us into the mountains, and we pulled over on a road that was probably private property, but warning signs didn't have much authority over us. We took a bin, gloves, and clippers from the trunk and began searching for mesquite wood that grew naturally in the foothills. There was a smoker grill at the compound, and Dafna was already at the grocery store picking up two giant slabs of beef ribs for us to smoke with wood we gathered.

Monica wore a miniskirt and flip-flops, but that didn't stop her from showing us how it was done or from correcting me when I presented her with a pile of mangled tumbleweed instead of mesquite. The gloves protected our hands from the thorns, but not our arms, and I had scratches along my wrists and below my elbows that quickly swelled. Mesquite was quite the territorial soldier.

Back at the compound, everyone drank beer while waiting for the meat to be ready. I monitored the levels on the smoker, adding more mesquite as needed to keep it going. Monica checked on me once, showed me how to read the thermometer, and then wandered off, in and out of the group on the patio, trusting me with our meal and her expensive grill.

I thought of those days early on in my marriage when we had a small round charcoal grill on the patio of our apartment. John refused to use lighter fluid and would instead struggle for more than an hour to get the chimney to stay lit and heat the coals. Every piece of chicken, every burger, brat, and rib, was over-seasoned when prepped and then overcooked on the grill, the edges charred, and the middle dry. John loved it. He gnawed through the blackened meat, while I cut around the inedible parts, smiling and nodding my appreciation that he—once again—insisted on doing the cooking.

When I cooked, the food was healthier, but John had been a smoker for so many years that the natural flavor of food was often lost on him. He leaned over the stove top, moving in so close to the pan that his nose practically grazed the food before he could smell it. I almost slapped his face away once, just a few months before we decided to separate and then divorce.

Late one night, I had been cooking in the biggest kitchen we ever had in a tiny house thirty minutes outside of Las Cruces that required me to drive through tunnels upon tunnels of pecan groves to get home every day. John came into the kitchen for another beer and asked questions about what we were having, how I had prepared it, what seasonings or oils had been used for flavor, what were we having for sides, and finally he stuck his nose in the chicken.

"I don't like meat that tastes like meat." He had the same expression on his face that he'd had when he tried to give me a curfew while out with my friends. At the time I ignored it and instead came home hours later to find him standing next to the back door, smoking in the dark, the light from the kitchen window illuminating his defeated disappointment.

In the kitchen, I raised my hand to slap his face away from the pan, but instead shoved him gently on the shoulder to ease him away.

At the residency, everyone trusted that I knew what I was doing, at least well enough to not interfere. The smoker needed more wood, and some of the larger mesquite branches needed to be snipped into pieces to fit. While trying to break them apart, a thorn slipped under my thumbnail and pierced the skin. There was no time to run for a bandage, no opportunity to step away and assess the damage. Instead, I pressed my finger against my thumb to quell the bleeding until the fire was burning hot enough again.

We smoked those ribs for almost three hours before they were ready to eat. It was well after dark before we stood around the picnic table and let the sauce cover our hands, our faces, and drip mercilessly onto our shirts. Nobody talked and nobody minded the red drips collecting on the metal tabletop in front of us. We could barely see the whites of each other's eyes under the pavilion, but there was just enough moonlight to see the piles of ribs stacked on two large platters. It was all the light we needed.

*

I woke up early. After two weeks of setting my own schedule in New Mexico, I didn't need an alarm. The courtyard was empty and quiet as I slipped out of my studio apartment, through the gate—taking care to not let it slam shut behind me—and walked down the gravel road. I wasn't certain where I was headed, except just in the direction of the mountains, then over a few blocks, and toward a yellow bus and small pop-up tent.

After I arrived, a man with longish red hair, though balding, and square bangs greeted me and told me his name, which I instantly forgot.

"Anyone riding with you today?"

"No," I said and handed him a folded ten dollar bill. "But it's not my first time on a river." I smiled to show confidence and because he didn't stop smiling at me. We made small talk until a few groups arrived, then we all boarded the bus and chugged along for six miles to the drop-off point. It was hot on those vinyl seats; the open windows barely circulated the already-warm air. The driver, Captain Bob, opened a can of Bud Light and sipped it as we bounce through turns, and the trailer hauling the tubes swayed behind us.

It was the last day of my residency, and I needed a break from too much time writing, too much time with the same people, too much time just an hour's drive away from the town of my marriage, but without a car, I hadn't been able to go back.

My ex-husband was in Utah doing whatever it was that ex-husbands do, and I was there, back in New Mexico, pushing a tube out into the Rio Grande and climbing into its center to float my way from morning into afternoon. The water was tranquil, trickling quietly along the bank, dark and full of mystery. The water was calm. Until it wasn't.

My head went under. I clawed at the lifejacket as it pressed into my throat, but I couldn't tell if my fingers were touching the jacket or the tube. Everything was confusing. Everything was changing shape. *Why had I gone for that rapid?* I admonished myself instead of focusing all of my energy on finding my way to the surface of the river to breathe.

Just breathe. *Follow the sun.* The sun seemed to be everywhere, though. A black sun, a bright sun. I had challenged the river, defied it. Had I done this on purpose? Perhaps I deserved it. Maybe it was because of John and Raul and Ryan and Jason, because I mistreated them all in my own way. I had gone at their hearts wondering what was the worst that could happen? Then I did whatever the hell I wanted. I knew better but did it anyway.

It was as though I was back on that snowy road, back in the driver's seat as the other car skidded toward me. There were two choices: let this kill me by doing nothing or save myself by doing something. The near-accident was not the only time I'd been given such a choice. There were so many moments, just moments, where I had resigned myself to quit living. Death wasn't something I would, or could, bring on myself. I didn't imagine what it would be like to die; I didn't try to put myself in the mindset of others who had ended their lives. No, it wasn't like that. I wasn't *proactive*. It was simply that I had considered not being *reactive*. What if I just didn't fight back? What if I just let it happen?

No, I decided. *I did not come to the desert to die.*

Gripping the lifejacket with both hands, I pulled it down toward my body, not away as I had been trying to do, and used my legs to kick

Melissa Grunow

myself to the surface. I emerged to the desert sun as the riverbank shifted from feral brush to walkways leading to adobe houses. The river had found its city.

I draped my arms over the tube and kicked myself to the side, but there was no shore. There were stone steps leading down from houses, docks that extended out to the water, posted signs that warned, "No wake area." Tall sea grass, deep black muck, and steep eroded walls lined the water's edge. Finally, I pushed myself up onto algae-covered rocks and climbed back onto the tube. The next time the tube approached some rapids, I stayed to the right and gently coasted over the rutted water.

Colorful ribbons decorated the brush along the river's edge to indicate the end of the journey. Climbing up the tiny beach and back to the pop-up tent, I left duality and oblivion in the river among the broken glass stuck between boulders. Obscurity was the day's lesson.

Chapter Fifteen

I stood in front of the stage, leaned against a giant speaker, and watched her: Anna Nalick. There she was, up on the stage directly in front of me, accompanied by a keyboard player to her left and nothing more. I was at the concert alone, without friends, just a mile from my home, my one square inch of comfort. Since that previous summer when I dumped myself in the river, I had forced myself to grow accustomed to being alone. The only way for me to learn to live was to learn to live with myself.

Most people stayed in their seats at the back of the venue, and I would have been among them if the middle-aged lesbian who sent her friend over to hit on me didn't continue to glance in my direction during the chorus of each song. Finally, I ditched my empty beer bottle, to the front, and watched a show that was worth quadruple what I paid.

During the last song, two drunk girls came out of nowhere and danced like hippies next to me, singing along with Anna at the top of their lungs. Didn't they know it was my private concert? I was annoyed by their presence but didn't allow it to distract me from my sheer infatuation with being right in front of her as she swayed to her music on the stage.

After the show, I waited in line for the meet-and-greet, where she agreed to not only sign my CD and concert ticket, but to have a photo taken together as well. The two drunk girls from the stage were in line in front of me, or at least they wanted to be. A man with dark hair slicked to the side wearing a black leather jacket chatted them up while his wife or girlfriend hung on him and smiled along.

The drunk girls thought maybe they could cut in line since they had become acquainted with leather jacket guy at the bar, but he laughed them off and shooed them away. He was short, not much taller than me, and the girl hanging on him towered over his head in her stiletto heels like a shaky baby giraffe.

I stood back a little and studied my CD, my hands, my cell phone, anything to avoid looking up. My lesbian stalker from earlier in the night was with her friends in front of leather-jacket guy and baby-giraffe lady, and I didn't want to draw attention to myself and start the staring all over again. Leather-jacket guy turned slightly toward his giraffe girlfriend, and I saw the sneering grin of his smile, how his lips pulled back and revealed his teeth up to his gums. The flickering lights of the venue angled toward him so that he was in a spotlight for a moment, and I took a step back with a gasp.

Jason.

At least it looked like him, or how Jason would look in his late forties, early fifties, and giraffe lady looked how I might in another ten or fifteen years if I had stayed with him. The man was Jason's future doppelganger, and not just in appearance. He had the same crass humor and tone in his voice, he came across as funnier than he actually was, and was successful in getting women to laugh at his jokes because he was small and appeared non-threatening.

It had been more than a year since I saw Jason, not since the day in the parking lot when I kissed him good-bye. I hadn't thought about him in almost as long, especially because Linda moved to a new position in a different building, so we didn't see each other much anymore. It had been months since I picked apart the things he had said to me, his abusive comments and his cruel accusations.

I managed to move on from him quickly because I had been with someone like Raul whose words continued to echo in the canyons of my memory, creeping up unexpectedly and fading away slowly. Jason's attempts at manipulation and control and his prevalence toward abuse were easily recognizable. Unlucky for Jason, I had the strength to stand up to him, to tell him not to speak to me that way, and to stand by my insistence.

Leather-jacket guy didn't notice me staring at him. Instead, he focused his attention on acting as a pedestal to keep giraffe-lady upright. They were having fun, but they didn't know the significance of the moment. Nothing mattered to them besides each other.

Finally, I accepted what I felt to be truth: I was so glad he wasn't my future any longer.

When it was my turn to meet Anna Nalick, I set aside my shy hesitation, mustered up all the courage that I could find within me, marched up to her and said, "I have to tell you the story of your album. I used to live in New Mexico, and after graduate school, I had a job that required me to drive all over the state as a program evaluator. I would listen to your CD on full volume with the windows down, singing out as loud as I could. So now, when I hear your music, I feel the heat of the desert and see mountains and red sand and rocks and cactuses and tumbleweeds."

I stopped to breathe and realized I had nothing else to say. Although I was a little embarrassed and a little sheepish, I felt hopeful. Maybe she would get it. Maybe she would understand.

Her eyes watered a little as I spoke, dancing along with my words, her face unchanged.

"I love to hear that," she said. "Obviously, my writing means something to me, but when I hear what it means to other people, well, I can't tell you how that feels." Then she took my CD from my hand and wrote, "Thank you for the story," before signing her name across the cover.

The next morning, I loaded Duke into the car along with a duffle bag and drove across Michigan to Illinois to visit my parents for the weekend. I couldn't shake the feeling of seeing such a twin image of Jason after having not given much thought to him in so long. It left me feeling rattled and anxious.

Our courtship had been so fast, that the few short months we were together seemed like a year or more in any other relationship. The early expressions of love, the time he spent sharing my bed, the moments of kindness and overwhelming generosity, the time he took me to jewelry store after jewelry store in the mall to look at engagement rings, finally stomping his foot and scoffing that none of them were good enough for my finger, even though I wasn't yet convinced that an engagement was my endgame. All of those moments haunted my thoughts throughout the weekend.

Driving back to Michigan on Sunday, I stopped at the Welcome Center just within the state line and took Duke out on his leash. I thought about leaving my cell phone in the car but decided to take it with me and distract myself with social media updates while Duke sniffed the ground to track every unfamiliar smell.

My feet stopped short, unable to continue forward, and the leash dropped from my hand. Duke turned to look at me, knowing he was supposed to sit when I stopped walking, but not certain as to what to do if no one was holding onto him. I wanted to say something, to speak out loud to someone, but there was no one to hear the words.

"Jason is dead."

In the year since we had broken up, he had met someone new, a younger woman named Meaghan, who lavished him with attention and clung to him like giraffe-lady had to leather-jacket guy at the concert. She loved him, found him hilarious, appreciated him in a way that I never could, and within that year they had bought a condo together and were talking about marriage. They had a housewarming party scheduled in a few more weeks when they were going to announce their engagement.

Instead, Jason went to a party he wasn't planning to attend. He gave into the relentless requests that he "just stop by" for "just a little while," and even though it was late, he finally went. After all, he wanted those friends to attend their engagement party. Meaghan stayed home. This happened sometimes, Linda told me, where he would go out and she wouldn't, and it worked for them. Instead of joining him, Meaghen asked him to call her if he needed a ride home later; that is if he decided to not stay at the party.

"Somebody is going to die tonight," his text message read, and he quickly laughed it off and corrected "die" to "drive."

"Somebody is going to drive tonight."

When it got late, Meaghan went to bed. Jason stayed at the party. He drank. Then he probably did other things, things that none of us knew about. They were experiments we never imagined him participating in, circles of substances that crossed the nameless and experimental threshold of "puff, puff, pass."

As the party came to an end, he sat down on the couch and texted his fiancé, "I love you more than life."

Then he slumped to the side, fell asleep, and never woke up again.

*

I planned to go to the funeral but couldn't. Instead, I went to work that day, typed content into evaluation forms and reviewed them with direct reports. I answered phone calls and emails, dealt with student issues, faculty issues, and policy issues. After a while, the phone calls went to voicemail, and I worked with my door closed for part of the afternoon. I walked up and down and up and down the stairs to avoid the suffocation of staying at my desk, climbing until my hamstrings burned only to climb some more.

When morning turned into afternoon and it was time to leave for the funeral, I couldn't do it. His family was there to mourn him, and I didn't want to be a ghost from his past. After all, as Linda said, "We knew a different kind of Jason." They needed to grieve the Jason they knew, not the one I remembered. We had both loved him, but my love for him ended; theirs never would.

In the evening, I sat on my bed and stared ahead at the wall, Duke's head on my lap as I moved my fingers through his fur. The dog was patient with me. He was quiet in a way that was uncharacteristic of his high-energy nature. When my hand stopped moving, he tilted his head upward toward me, his large brown eyes compelling me to continue.

The windows were open as spring was back again after a brutally cold and snowy winter, Michigan's worst on record. I heard a distant whistle outside my window, three short and one long, and the chugging of a locomotive along the tracks, a bell ringing as it passed through town. The train whistle was always there when I needed something to coax me to keep moving forward, but I had nowhere to go from this.

Did Jason choose to sit down on that couch and die? Or did he simply choose to not save himself? I thought of myself on the river, and realized we weren't so different. We both had a life; we both had a breath. I chose to fight for mine. Jason's left with the sending of a text and settling into the corner of a couch. What if it had been different? What kind of Jason was he? Would he have made me into a different person? What would I have made for myself? They were questions that I couldn't answer.

His body was small. It was small and it was battered from the inside out. To me, his heart felt small, though only in the end. He couldn't accept the vulnerability that love required. Even up until his breathing turned shallow, he believed himself invincible. Oblivion was his lesson.

Ultimately, I didn't know what kind of person he was. And maybe I didn't have to know. Those memories belonged to his family. For us, though, we had our moments of kindness and of warmth. They were moments that gave me hope his outward clown-around persona was just a performance, that he wasn't as off-putting as I perceived. There was no speaking of it, though, because there was no way to make sense of it.

The train whistle blew again, and Duke raised his head to look at me, startled by the noise that should have already passed. I scratched him between the ears and he settled back down with a sigh. Curling in next to him, I closed my eyes, and let the evening take us both.

Acknowledgements

For their feedback on drafts and content development as the memoir took shape, I thank Chelsey Clammer, Robert Root, Amina Cain, and my classmates in the National University Master of Fine Arts program. Gratitude also extends to Leslie Jamison, Dinty W. Moore, and Kate Hopper for support and encouraging words. Of course, this book would not be possible without Douglas Owen of Tumbleweed Books for taking a chance on an unknown writer and his scrupulous feedback during the editing process.

I owe gratitude to Starry Night Programs and Antioch Writers Weekend Retreat for the writing residencies that enabled me to finish the early drafts of the manuscript. I also thank the coordinators of the River Teeth Nonfiction Conference, Creative Nonfiction Conference, and the Detroit Working Writers Annual Conference for connecting me with other writers and giving me a chance to talk about my project to anyone who would listen. Those sessions and conversations helped shape the book so I could achieve my vision.

I am humbled by the editors and readers of The Quotable, Eunoia Review, Yemassee, 94 Creations Literary Review, Writing Disorder, Narrative Northeast, Behemoth Review, Mulberry Fork Review, New Mexico Review, Buck Off Magazine, and The Chiron Review, in which some excerpts of content and ideas from this book originally appeared. I am humbled that they chose to include my work in their journals and appreciate their readers who sent me kind words along the way.

Special thanks to Glen Stewart, Michelle Hier, Joe Leuenberger, Austin Chapman, and Nick Paauwe who all gave me total freedom with trust and valiance to include them. To my "work wife" Janel Mills, thank you for not allowing me to lose sight of my vision. Most importantly, endless gratitude to Chris Ahern who understands when I need to put writing first. Thank you for showing me what true partnership can be—an adventure with no itinerary, a River City we can realize together.

About the Author

Melissa Grunow's writing has appeared in *Creative Nonfiction, River Teeth, New Plains Review, Blue Lyra Review, Temenos,* and *Yemassee,* among many others.

An award-winning writer, Melissa was a semi-finalist for the 2015 DISQUIET International Literary Lisbon Writing Program in Portugal and a two-time recipient of the Detroit Working Writers creative nonfiction prize.

Melissa holds a Bachelor of Science in English-creative writing and journalism from Central Michigan University, a Master of Arts in English from New Mexico State University, and a Master of Fine Arts in Creative Writing with distinction from National University.

She lives and writes in Detroit, Michigan. *Realizing River City* is her first book. Visit her website at www.melissagrunow.com.